ISRAEL'S EDGE

The Story of the IDF's Most Elite Unit – Talpiot

JASON GEWIRTZ

gefen גפן
publishing house בית הוצאה לאור
JERUSALEM ◆ NEW YORK   Est. 1981

Cover Design: Joe Potter
Typesetting: Irit Nachum

ISBN: 978-965-229-713-6

7 9 8 6

Gefen Publishing House Ltd.
6 Hatzvi Street
Jerusalem 94386, Israel
972-2-538-0247
orders@gefenpublishing.com

Gefen Books
11 Edison Place
Springfield, NJ 07081
516-593-1234
orders@gefenpublishing.com

www.gefenpublishing.com

Printed in Israel

Send for our free catalog

Library of Congress Cataloging-in-Publication Data

Names: Gewirtz, Jason, author.
Title: Israel's edge : Talpiot, the IDF's most elite unit / Jason Gewirtz.
Description: Jerusalem : Gefen Publishing House Ltd., [2015]
Identifiers: LCCN 2015017950 | ISBN 9789652297136
Subjects: LCSH: Tokhnit Talpiyot (Israel) | Israel. Tseva haganah
    le-Yi?sra?el—Officers—Training of.
Classification: LCC U660.I75 G49 2015 | DDC 355.3/43—dc23 LC
record available at http://lccn.loc.gov/2015017950

This book is dedicated to:

My father, the most honorable person I've ever known

My mother, the most selfless person I've ever known

My brother, the strongest person I've ever known

My wife, the most caring and wonderful person I've ever known

My two girls...be whoever you want to be, but be good and do good

To all of Talpiot's past and future graduates, and to all the men
and women who have served in the Israeli army;
you not only guard a nation's border, you protect a people.

CONTENTS

INTRODUCTION

Each year fifty thousand Israelis reach draft age. And each year staffers in the Israel Defense Forces' manpower offices start pointing young men and women in different directions.

To tank units. To the infantry. To the air force. To the navy. To artillery divisions. To special units designed to educate the underprivileged. To pioneering units, engineering, intelligence; the list goes on and on. Men are assigned to units for at least the next three years; women, at least the next twenty months.

This is a country that needs a strong fighting force perhaps more than any nation in the world, and the army is idolized by its youth. In the years before their induction, motivated Israeli teenagers jockey for position, boosting their high school grades and preparing for special IDF induction tests. Hoping to earn invitations to enlist in the units they've set their sights on, thousands of young Israelis even sign up for physical fitness coaching and private pre-army training in order to prepare themselves for the rigorous physical IDF exams that will decide who is sent where.

It used to be the air force that had first pick of these capable young men and women. They needed the brightest and most physically fit to fly complicated fighter jets, large transport planes and heavily armed silent attack helicopters – the fighting force that makes up the long arm of the Israeli Air Force. It was rare that anyone would say no to the air force. Like American boys who dreamed of becoming a baseball star, many Israeli boys hoped to grow up and serve their country by piloting an F16.

If the air force wasn't your goal, or if your eyesight wasn't perfect, another highly desired spot was a place in Israel's celebrated elite commando units such as Sayeret Matkal or the paratroopers, with their distinctive red boots that symbolize to everyone just how tough you are and how dedicated you are to your country.

But in 1979 something began to change. While the air force and top ground units were still, and always will be, a very high priority for Israel, another unit – a secret unit – took over as top priority for the IDF.

Soldiers picked for this unit aren't expected to fight like ordinary soldiers. Instead, they are expected to learn. They are selected for an ultra-competitive, grueling, fast-paced program designed to give them the best educational and military training possible.

Their teachers are some of the world's top minds in mathematics, physics and computer science, as well as some of Israel's top strategic leaders from the army, navy and air force. The end game is to produce soldiers with great military and scientific backgrounds who are trained to think like nobody else in the world.

They do not enlist like every other soldier in the IDF for three years or twenty months. They sign up for a full decade. Because the program is so intense, almost one in four of these bright minds originally selected won't make it through the program.

Graduates of the unit are expected to accumulate massive amounts of knowledge and apply it directly to help Israel's deterrence shield, to help Israel's intelligence services and to make the army, navy and air force stronger in any conflict.

This small, select group is expected to change the way Israel does battle. The country is counting on them to give the Israel Defense Forces an eternal edge over its enemies by developing the weapons and military hardware of the future.

Since this unit became a part of the IDF, no other group of soldiers has had such a profound impact on Israel – on Israel's defense doctrine, on how Israel's weapons are developed and how they're used.

The military advantage these special graduates gave Israel didn't end when their army service was over. Those who left the army often took what they did for the IDF and applied it to the Israeli economy, creating hundreds of billions of dollars of wealth and tens of thousands of jobs in Israel and beyond. They have dramatically helped give Israel an edge on the battlefield and in global business.

This is their story, the story of Talpiot.

CHAPTER 1

A DEVASTATING FORCE FOR CHANGE

O ctober 1973: "The source" tells his Mossad handler in London that war between Israel and its Arab neighbors is imminent. He's been wrong before, but with all of the other signs on the Syrian and Egyptian sides of the border, it looks like this could be the real thing.

Agents from Britain to Israel are buzzing as they work their way up the chain to the director of the Mossad, Zvi Zamir. He flies to London immediately to meet with "the source" – a man now believed to be Ashraf Marwan, the son-in-law of former Egyptian president Gamal Abdel Nasser. The Mossad and Israel's other intelligence agencies had their doubts about "the source," suspecting him of being a double agent. To this day the truth has not been revealed.

Zamir believes the information is credible and hopes the wheels of Israel's war machine will begin to move forward.

He is able to convince Israel's Prime Minister Golda Meir and Minister of Defense Moshe Dayan of the impending attack.

Despite having that crucial information, Israel's leadership decides not to act – fearing it will be blamed for firing the first shot and that Israel will thus lose critical support from the United States. Secretary of State Henry Kissinger has warned Israel's leaders – including Prime Minister Meir – that if war should break out, Israel had best make sure it isn't the one who starts the fighting.

At noon, October 5, Israeli military intelligence reports state, "The probability that the Egyptians intend to renew fighting is low. There is no change in our estimate of Syrian intentions."

October 6, 1973 – Yom Kippur, the tenth of the Hebrew month of Tishrei, 5734. At 2:00 PM, Egypt attacks Israel. Syria follows suit a few minutes later.

Israel is caught off guard as Egypt begins its assault, crossing the Suez Canal, which had separated Egyptian and Israeli forces since 1967. The pace of Egypt's advance across the canal picks up speed amid cries broadcast from loudspeakers on Egypt's side of the canal, *"Allahu akbar! Allahu akbar!"* (God is great! God is great!). Israeli troops stationed along the Bar Lev Line – constructed as an "unbreakable defense" against Egypt after the war in 1967 – prepare to defend their lives and their country against the onslaught. For many Israelis trapped on the Bar Lev Line, this will be their final day.

In the north, Syrian tanks pour across the border that had marked the cease-fire line established six years before. Syrian commando forces are helicoptered to Mount Hermon, taken by Israel in 1967. Syrian fighters and bombers fly sortie after sortie, bombarding soft and hard Israeli targets.

Confusion reigns from the northern tip of Israel in the Golan Heights to the Sinai desert in the south. Field commanders desperately try to stop the simultaneous advances from the north and south.

Government leaders in Jerusalem are stunned into silence and worse, inaction, while army leaders in Tel Aviv initially dismiss reports of the attacks as exaggerations. It is impossible to believe their Arab enemies are capable of launching such swift and effective incursions. Didn't these same Israeli officers brilliantly thrash six Arab armies just a few years earlier? Defense Minister Moshe Dayan, the highest ranking military official in the country, leads his closest advisers to believe that there is no problem; the situation is under control and the Israel Defense Forces will quickly turn the tide.

Sirens blast throughout Israel on this, the holiest day on the Jewish calendar. Nearly all Israelis, religious or not, mark Yom Kippur by forgoing work, attending synagogue services, fasting, praying and contemplating. Bewildered Israelis stream out of their homes and synagogues. They gather around radios waiting for news, anxiously listening for the codes that will instruct reserve units where to gather.

(Israel's military brass had always contended it would need forty-eight hours to mobilize reserves, the backbone of the Israeli army. And intelligence agencies had always promised that giving forty-eight hours' notice would not be a problem. Dead wrong.)

Israeli reservists and volunteers commandeer cars and buses, hitching rides. Citizens beyond army age hastily arrange carpools to get soldiers to the places where hundreds of units have been told to assemble for orders.

As the confusion in Israel grows, traffic backs up on the

roads. Israel approaches panic mode while Egypt and Syria approach the first-day goals they set for themselves during the months of planning that led to "The October War," as it is referred to in Arabic.

Forty-eight hours into the fighting, Israel is suffering unprecedented losses on the battlefield and the political leadership is having a hard time coming to grips with the turn of events. Sobering intelligence reports reach Dayan detailing heavy losses and reports of Israeli positions overrun. Dayan's confidence evaporates.

Egypt now has hundreds of tanks and thousands of troops on the Israeli side of the Suez Canal – an unthinkable scenario just a few days earlier. In the north, the Syrian advance continues. Syria's tanks close in on the edge of a plain that stares down on Haifa and the rest of the Israeli coast.

As Dayan finally realizes the level of danger to his country, he gives chilling assessments of the situation to his inner circle and to other high-ranking members of the government. In his epic book *The Yom Kippur War*, Abraham Rabinovich writes about an off-the-record meeting between Dayan and the editors of Israel's newspapers in an attempt to level with the nation. Sources told Rabinovich that Dayan said, "Israel might be forced to withdraw deep into the Sinai…. The world has seen that we are not stronger than the Egyptians. The aura, and the political and military advantage of it being known that Israel is stronger than the Arabs and that it would beat them if they go to war, this has not been proven here" (page 270).

A shaken Dayan is set to deliver a similar message to the nation that night. But one of the newspaper editors fears that the general will further erode morale and alarm everyone in the country. He reaches Prime Minister Meir and advises her to have another high-ranking military officer make the address to the nation.

***

How did this fiasco happen? When the Egyptian surprise attack began on October 6, there were only about a dozen Israeli tanks protecting the road that led from the Sinai straight into Tel Aviv. How did Israel – mighty Israel, which had so thoroughly routed its enemies in the Six-Day War of 1967 – fall to such a low state of preparedness only six years later?

In the years between the Six-Day War and the start of the Yom Kippur War, Israel was engaged in a constant war of attrition with Egypt and Syria. There was daily shelling from behind the Arab lines targeting Israel's military on the 1967 border and residential communities not far from those lines, especially in the north of Israel.

Many nations that previously had supplied arms to Israel cut off arms shipments due to Arab threats. This was especially true of France, Israel's main weapons supplier before 1967. The French were told that if they supplied Israel with weapons, the Arabs would cut off oil shipments to France. The United States picked up some of the slack, but not all of it, and Israel was left without a major weapons supplier.

At the same time, Arab nations – especially Egypt and Syria – were showered with arms by the Soviet Union, as the USSR tried to strengthen its hold in this complicated, energy rich, and critical part of the world. In addition to its immense success in resupplying their armies, Egypt and Syria made strides in training crews to man new weapons systems and rapidly advanced in planning strategy.

All this happened amid an air of complacency in Israel. The country was still resting and satisfied with itself after the massive victory in 1967; citizens, army officers and the government thought there was no way Israel could be defeated.

That smugness came to a swift end when war broke out in 1973. In the opening days of fighting, Israel lost forty-nine planes (compared to forty-six planes during the entire Six-Day War). By the time the Yom Kippur war ended in late October, Israel had lost almost a fifth of its air force. Almost all of those planes lost by the Israeli Air Force were shot down by Soviet-made surface-to-air missiles. The Russian SAMs were so proficient that Israeli pilots would call them "flying telephone poles," alluding to the wires that could snag a low-flying fighter jet – wires that were impossible to evade at a low altitude.

Those Soviet SAMs were so new and sophisticated, no air force in the world could dodge them. The Israeli military came to the shocking realization that the IAF was no longer in complete control of the skies. Israel's defense doctrine had been built on tanks and airplanes, and both were being soundly defeated by new technology owned by the Arabs.

Air defense wasn't the only area where Arab nations had advanced their fighting technologies. Arab foot soldiers defeated Israeli tank columns with brand new, portable, AT-3 Sagger wire-guided anti-tank missiles. (The Russians call them 9K11 Malyutka missiles.) They were carried into the Sinai desert by Egyptian troops in suitcase-sized containers. Before the shooting started on October 6, Egyptian special forces passed through the Israeli frontline on the Suez Canal with their new and deadly cargo.

Israel's high command had some knowledge of the Sagger, learned from American fighting experiences in Vietnam. But high-ranking Israeli officers did not believe Arab fighters would be strong enough or brave enough to confront Israeli tanks. They knew that in one-on-one battle an Israeli tank crew could usually defeat its Egyptian or Syrian counterpart. Israel's tank crews were generally better educated and better trained than Arab crews; moreover Israel's tanks were more accurate and could fire from a longer distance.

But they had not considered the Egyptian army's ability to use the sophisticated Saggers, and Israeli tank crews were caught totally unprepared. After stealthily crossing the canal, the Egyptians set up shop, hiding behind sand dunes and setting up traps that would easily ensnare formidable Israeli tank units.

Military experts later confirmed that "the Sagger operator would find it much easier to hit a tank than the other way around, and at ranges that matched the tanks" (Rabinovich, page 36). The large Israeli tanks made inviting targets for Sagger marksmen: Egyptian specialists would lock onto Israeli armor more than a mile away, fire and destroy tank after tank with deadly accuracy. In contrast, Israelis searching for Sagger crews in the vast desert sand could rarely locate them. This new element to the ground war would cost Israel dozens of tanks in the opening days of fighting.

In the crucial early days of fighting, it became clear that counter attack and reinforcement of Israeli troops would be impossible. Israeli tank reinforcements positioned ten miles away from the canal were easy prey for those hidden Sagger crews. When reserve tank forces tried to push forward to Israeli positions along the canal, they were picked off one by one.

Communications failed as well. Less than forty-eight hours after the war began, with eyewitnesses reporting Syria and Egypt were using machine guns to kill scores of Israelis captured in the opening hours of the war, Defense Minister

Dayan found himself having trouble getting through to commanders on the ground.

At the same time, the air force was planning an operation to try to destroy Egypt's Soviet made anti-aircraft batteries. Minutes before the mission was set to launch, Dayan contacted Benny Peled, commander of the Israeli Air Force, and called it off, diverting all planes to the north to stop the Syrian advance. His logic was that there was only sand in the Sinai between Israel proper and Egyptian tanks in the south. In the north, Israeli civilians were about to be in Syrian range: without the air force, those population centers, including Haifa, were doomed.

During the 5:00 AM conversation with Peled on October 7, Dayan said, "If our planes are not attacking by noon the Syrians will reach the Jordan Valley." Then for the first time Dayan used a phrase that he would repeat in the coming days to the dismay of all who heard him. "The Third Temple," he told Peled, "is in danger" (Rabinovich, page 175).

"The Third Temple" was, and is still, code to many representing modern-day Israel. The first two Holy Temples in Jerusalem were destroyed in ancient times; the first by the Babylonians in the year 586 BCE, the second by the Romans in the year 70 CE. To many secular Israelis, as well as Jews all over the world, today's Israel is the "Third Temple."

The intelligence failures that led to Israel's early problems in the Yom Kippur War were dramatic and are still referred to today, more than forty years after the war, but the war wasn't a total surprise to everyone in Israel. Some intelligence officers had seen signs that war was imminent. Soviet advisers and diplomats had moved their families out of the country in the days before October 6. There were widespread troop mobilizations in both Egypt and Syria; Arab troops were on the move, en masse.

There was also somewhat confusing evidence that the Egyptian and Syrian units mobilizing near the front lines were getting instructions to carry out "training" exercises. The idea was to move troops into position, but allow Israeli spies and communication eavesdroppers to believe it was for the purpose of training only – not war. However, a more careful Israeli inspection would have allowed the Israelis to see that those troops weren't actually carrying out exercises at all: they were simply preparing for an invasion. If all this weren't enough, there was a direct warning from Jordan's King Hussein to Prime Minister Meir in person during a secret face-to-face meeting.

In modern warfare, the side that fires first often has the upper hand. Waiting to be attacked is especially risky for a tiny country like Israel, which is only sixty miles wide at its broadest point. At its narrowest point, Israel is roughly ten miles wide. Even a moderate thrust by the enemy could cut the country in half in the first hours of any war.

Of course, Prime Minister Meir knew all of this, but decided to wait and hope for the best rather than risk diplomatic blowback, especially from the United States. She had been assured over and over by her military advisors – including revered Defense Minister Dayan – that if war were to break out, Israel would be able to smash its enemies again as the country had done in 1967.

When the shooting stopped and cease-fire agreements were signed three weeks later, Israeli citizens, the government and army woke up to a bitter reality. They were not invincible.

Two thousand six hundred fifty-six Israeli soldiers had

been killed. Almost nine thousand others lay wounded. The backbone of the IDF – its formidable tank force – had lost two hundred of its three hundred tanks in the Sinai in the first twenty-four hours of the war. Scores of Israel's fighter planes were gone.

The Arab armies had not only caught up, but had surpassed Israel in technology, subterfuge, strategy and operational capability. Israel also lost in an area that was unforgivable: they lost the intelligence war.

The trauma of the Yom Kippur War and the realistic fear that another war could mean extinction lingered. In the war's aftermath, the entire military establishment and political leadership were forced to resign. The prime minister and Defense Minister Dayan both left eight months after the war ended. Key players in intelligence and in the IDF were ousted.

For a nation born out of the ashes of the Holocaust to be threatened in such a way has a deep, scarring and lasting impact that affects every aspect of public life. A country of this size, surrounded by so many enemies with much larger armies and with suppliers like the Soviet Union, simply could not risk another war such as this. For years, Israel existed in a state of quiet tension and nobody really knew how to return to the sense of security most of the population had felt just after the Six-Day War.

Everyone knew that Israel would never have the numbers compared to Egypt, Syria, Iraq, Jordan, Lebanon, Saudi Arabia, Iran, Algeria, Libya and Sudan. As the deck forever will be stacked against Israel quantitatively, it became clearer than ever that Israel needed a qualitative advantage.

It was not long after the devastating Yom Kippur War that two professors at Hebrew University had an idea to give

Israel that qualitative edge it so desperately needed (and still needs today) to survive. Their goal was to rearm Israel with enterprising minds, a weapon no army could defeat or suppress. Those minds would supply Israel with advanced weapons ahead of anyone in the world.

But the professors' idea went beyond weapons. The concept was also to train those young minds to come up with new and better ways to monitor the enemy and to outsmart it.

The inspired proposal wouldn't just help fortify Israel for the next war. Their innovation gave Israel the lead it maintains today, four decades after the Yom Kippur War of 1973, the edge Israel will have over its enemies for decades to come.

CHAPTER 2

TALPIOT'S FOUNDING FATHERS

When the air-raid sirens began on October 6, 1973, Hebrew University professor of physics Shaul Yatziv knew the government would never call for a mock air raid on Yom Kippur. Something awful and unthinkable was happening.

Most Israelis had heard word of threats coming from Egypt and Syria, but like the government and the army, the civilians in the cities, villages and kibbutzim throughout the country knew little about Arab intentions. But when the silence of Yom Kippur was broken by siren blasts, and radio announcers calmly but urgently began reading the codes to mobilize reservists, it could mean only one thing: war.

Armed conflict was not new to Yatziv. Born in pre-state Palestine in 1927, he had lived through war and the threat of sudden violence from the day he was born. Following the declaration of Israel's independence in May 1948, he served in the first Jewish army assembled in two millennia.

Yatziv was a full professor at Hebrew University, part of

the university's Faculty of Natural Sciences; in 1973 he was conducting research on optical lasers and spectroscopy, the study of how matter reacts to radiated energy and vice versa.

Like everyone else in Israel, Yatziv was shocked by the Yom Kippur War and its ramifications. At forty-six, he was too old to make a difference as a soldier, but he had another idea, an idea that would give Israel a real edge going forward. He knew that he would need to develop his concept and collaborate with others to make it a reality. He thought of Professor Felix Dothan, a colleague at Hebrew University with whom he had shared his research over the past five years. Their focus on lasers and potential future applications had been promising.

But on Yom Kippur 1973, Professor Felix Dothan was far from the turmoil in Israel. On loan to the University of California-Irvine from Hebrew University, he was personally safe, but quite agitated. His homeland was under attack and he worried about his family and friends.

In most countries, residents under attack run away from the fighting. But when war breaks out in Israel, Israelis living abroad often run toward the fighting. They return from wherever they're living, working or vacationing. When the war broke out in 1973, international carriers cancelled all service to the Middle East, but El Al flights were filled with Israelis rushing to get home to help, to serve and to fight.

Professor Dothan was almost fifty years old in 1973. The country didn't need him in the army; it was more important for reservists of fighting age to have those airline seats. He would sit this war out, stranded in Southern California, left to nervously follow developments by reading newspapers and watching the evening news. He would have to wait patiently for word on the fate of his loved ones, including his son Yoav, who had joined the army at the age of seventeen, just two months before the war broke out. Usually soldiers aren't eligible to join until the age of eighteen, but because of Yoav's academic acumen and with his father's written consent, he was allowed to enlist early.

He was proud of his son's patriotism; it was the mark of a true Israeli. For unlike Shaul Yatziv, Felix Dothan was not a native of Israel. He was born Felix Deutsch in Zagreb, Yugoslavia, in 1924.

He had seen the dark side of life as a European Jew in his youth. Shortly after Yugoslavia had been occupied by the Germans, Felix and his classmates were told that the next day they were to assemble in the forest, rather than report to school. Felix's father refused to give his permission and Felix stayed home. They later learned that Nazis and their Yugoslavian collaborators had shot four hundred of his classmates to death.

That wasn't the only time Felix narrowly escaped death. Later, he was arrested along with his family by the Nazis, but managed to avoid deportation to Auschwitz due to the family's wealthy connections. Hidden by gentiles till the end of the war, he finished high school and started at the University of Zagreb, studying electrical engineering.

But a resurgent wave of anti-Semitism in Yugoslavia – and the realistic fear of being stuck behind the Soviet Union's Iron Curtain forever – propelled his family to move to Palestine while they still could. They arrived in 1948.

The War of Independence against seven invading Arab nations was raging. The profound impact of his narrow escapes from the hands of anti-Semites evoked his deep loyalty to the newly emerging Jewish nation. Deutsch joined the army and worked his way up the ladder to lieutenant colonel in the Israel

Defense Forces. After the cease-fire in 1949, he scratched out a living as a fisherman while continuing his studies in engineering and physics at the Technion in Haifa, graduating in 1951. (The Technion is Israel's version of the Massachusetts Institute of Technology in the United States.)

He immediately took a position at the precursor to Israel's now-famous Rafael Advanced Defense Systems in Jerusalem. The exact nature of his job remains classified, but it involved advancing the production, testing and manufacturing of new weapons for the army.

He carried that experience to a new position, teaching and researching at Hebrew University in Jerusalem. Hebrew U. is an auspicious place for a researcher; one of its founders was the celebrated physicist Albert Einstein, and it had the backing of philosopher Martin Buber, psychoanalyst Sigmund Freud and Israel's first president, Chaim Weizmann. Along with the Technion, it became the backbone of education in Palestine soon after opening its doors in 1925.

Enjoying a gratifying career, he continued his research in Switzerland, later returning with his young family to Jerusalem and Hebrew University's new physics lab. There he worked with electrified gas and plasma, which has many civilian and military applications. After completing his doctorate in 1965, he hit the road again, accepting a position as a visiting professor in Geneva's Institute for European Nuclear Research. There he specialized in working on calculations regarding magnetic fields, design and lasers.

A year after the pivotal Six-Day War of 1967, he became a senior lecturer at Hebrew University's Racah Institute of Physics and changed his name from the European-sounding Deutsch to a Hebraic version, Dothan.

After fulfilling his role as visiting professor at the University of California-Irvine in 1973, Professor Dothan made his way back home to Hebrew University. When he arrived, he was shocked to find the confident, happy country he had left in 1968 in the midst of a crisis. Israelis had lost trust in their government and in the military. The mood of his once-optimistic nation had turned decidedly pessimistic.

Professor Dothan wanted to help get his beloved Israel back on its feet; the question was how could he give such a gift to his nation. He knew the answer had to do with research and education, not military muscle, but even if he could come up with a viable plan, how could he get a military machine that's used to fighting wars with tanks and manpower to listen?

It was time to revive collaboration with Professor Yatziv. Together, they went to work, starting with a position paper to submit to Israel's top military officers. The paper states: "Concern for the fate of Israel and the wish to do the utmost to lower the number of casualties in future wars motivated us to submit a proposal that includes three important starting points that we do not have in existing research institutions."

Their starting point: "A firm recognition that the State of Israel must make an effort to develop totally innovative weapons that do not exist among the nations. This goal can only be obtained through human creativity, creativity that reaches its peak at the low biological age of the twenties. Inventive capability requires creative imagination, vast knowledge and deep understanding, but can be significantly encouraged by presenting challenges and creating a lively and motivating atmosphere where every effort and contribution will get encouragement from the surrounding environment. As one of the ways to reach this goal we propose a systematic and condensed effort to invent and develop new and efficient weapons, where new is defined as a weapon that is not in use in other armies, even in the armies of the superpowers. It is essential that the core of this program will be based on the most talented and dedicated people, who also possess the required background in the natural sciences and in the weapons technology."[1]

Their second point was to propose that the Israel Defense Forces would be directly responsible for the program and the people involved in it, specifically the Israeli Air Force.

As mentioned earlier, the air force was the most venerated branch of the IDF. They took only the best of the recruits, people who could be entrusted with the most expensive armaments in Israel's arsenal. They needed math skills, the ability to understand advanced physics and aeronautics, great test scores and the ability to think fast.

Part of Dothan and Yatziv's proposal was to change that doctrine, to push the brightest and most motivated soldiers to their newly conceived program.

In Israel most students don't graduate university until they are twenty-five years old due to three years of post–high school compulsory military service. If a student was accepted to Talpiot and then had to serve for eight years (as their plan stipulated), he would be behind his peers for far too long, putting him at a disadvantage throughout his career.

So point three of the original Talpiot proposal allowed for cadets to earn a Bachelor of Science degree in physics and mathematics (and later computer science as well), disciplines needed for engineers working on advanced weapons systems.

The original proposal called for cadets to earn those degrees

---

[1] IDF Archives.

in three years rather than the four given to ordinary students studying those subjects. After completing their studies, they would serve in the army for an additional five and a half years.

Getting started, however, wasn't so easy. Dothan and Yatziv needed the IDF brass on their side and not just the Ministry of Defense. They needed support from army and air force generals, other high ranking officers in different branches of the IDF and the all-important general staff.

Meeting with top generals, even in a country as small as Israel, isn't easy. In the 1970s, the army was Israel's most important institution, and many high-ranking officers didn't really want advice from professors or civilians.

For three years, Dothan and Yatziv met with the military brass, only to be denied at every turn. This was especially frustrating to Dothan because he had ties to two of Israel's top generals. Both General Haim Bar Lev and General David Elazar originally came from Zagreb. Both had distinguished themselves in previous wars, and Elazar was the nation's highest ranking officer, the chief of staff, during the Yom Kippur War. But hometown nostalgia was not enough to get Dothan through the door.

The truth was that in the wake of the Yom Kippur War, Elazar and all the top brass had troubles of their own that preoccupied them. Investigations into military fumbling during the war were being conducted by a special commission headed by Chief Justice of the Supreme Court Shimon Agranat.

The commission's final report was issued in January 1975, and the impact on Israel's political and military leadership was devastating. In addition to Golda Meir, many high-ranking officers – including Elazar – were forced to leave the army, along with several of their top deputies.

New leadership was brought in, but it would take time to rebuild the army's infrastructure. While the leadership was changing, the IDF was focused on quickly replacing armaments, tanks and fighter planes lost in the war. In the confusion, it is likely that nobody in the army had the time or the will to focus on a report from two outsiders.

In April 1977, with the country still reeling from the after effects of the Yom Kippur War, the Labor Party was swept out of office for the first time since the founding of the modern state in 1948. Menachem Begin, of the Likud Party, had led the opposition for decades, and now it was his turn to lead Israel.

Begin moved into the prime minister's office ready to make changes. Less than a year after taking office, Begin's defense minister, Ezer Weizman, appointed Rafael Eitan as chief of staff, Israel's highest ranking military officer. General Eitan was one of the Israeli officers credited with stopping the massive Syrian advance in the opening days of the Yom Kippur War. He had lost many of his soldiers in the fighting, but he escaped the war unscathed professionally.

He had come from a disadvantaged economic background, but he revered education and saw it as the key to improving the prospects of less advantaged Israeli youth. With Eitan's ascension to chief of staff, new life was pumped into Dothan and Yatziv's drive to form an elite educated unit in the army.

Their idea worked its way up the new and improved chain of command to the office of General Eitan. He was known to favor education, and because the structure of the army was changing, he had extra incentive to try new programs that would bear fruit in the years, decades and generations to come.

One day in 1978, after years of trying to break through the military's roadblocks, Dothan and Yatziv were finally called to deliver their proposal directly to Eitan. They arrived, proposal in hand, and spent a few minutes with the diminutive but imposing general. Then they were asked to wait in an exterior office.

General Eitan had his secretary ask Air Force Colonel Benjamin Machnes to come to his office immediately. A pilot in the early days of Israel, the highly capable Machnes rose up the ranks. After his flying days were over, he headed a school that taught air force personnel advanced physics and aeronautics. He reported directly to the head of the Israeli Air Force, General Benny Peled.

Eitan knew of Machnes's work at the air force school. Given permission by his commanding officer, Benny Peled, Machnes immediately reported to General Eitan. He described their meeting: "I opened the door and Raful (nickname for Raphael Eitan) was waiting with General Israel Tal, sitting there. Tal was our top tank general; he invented the Merkava.... I said, 'Hello, General Eitan, I'm Benji Machnes.' Eitan replied, 'Of course I know you.' He didn't even ask me to sit. He said, 'Outside my door are two professors. I think they have a good idea. Go and do it. That's all.'"

While Colonel Machnes was accepting the position as the army's first representative in this new joint venture with Israeli academia, Yatziv and Dothan waited anxiously. Machnes let himself out of the office and introduced himself to the professors. He then told them, "Your project has been accepted, let's get to work." Yatziv and Dothan looked incredulous. "That's it?" Machnes said yes, and the planning stages of Talpiot began right there outside of the chief of staff's office.

A short time later, General Ariel Sharon was named Minister of Defense. He was quickly brought up to speed on the project.

He told Machnes, "Benji, this is a good thing that you're doing." By Machnes's account, neither Sharon nor Eitan were particularly interested in becoming intimately involved in the program, but both were willing to gamble on it.

Professors Dothan and Yatziv were given a mandate to start, and were urged to launch their innovative program in just a few months' time. There was so much that had never been discussed, so many questions looming that would demand foresight, creativity, practicality and fortitude. They knew they would have to scramble to meet such a pressing deadline, but at last they were underway.

CHAPTER 3

FINDING THE SUPER SOLDIER

*T*he first thing the professors and Colonel Machnes had to do was name the program. For years, Dothan had been thinking of an appropriate name, and he suggested Talpiot. *Talpiot* has a few meanings in Hebrew, but its most popular definitions are "sturdy strongholds" or "tall turrets." In the biblical Song of Songs, *talpiot* appears as a metaphor for leadership. (Though not religiously observant, many of Israel's early leaders were aware of the historic national significance of the Jewish homeland and took pride in their new state's connection to the Bible. To this day, biblical references are commonplace in Israeli public venues.) The others agreed to the bold military title.

In order to launch the program in a matter of months, they had to quickly come up with a viable program, a syllabus, a home, a university partner, appropriate facilities, a way to find and recruit students, and a way to test potential applicants.

Dothan and Yatziv had both been insiders at Hebrew

22

University for some time. The army held meetings with several of the top universities in Israel including Hebrew University, Tel Aviv University and the Technion in Haifa.

There was outright rejection, at first. None of the three universities wanted soldiers on their campus. An early leader of Talpiot started to think the program would never get the backing of a university. One day, as he was speaking to a friend who was a secretary at Hebrew University, she asked him what was wrong. He told her the story and she exclaimed, "You haven't spoken to the right person!" Two minutes later, she came back with a vice president of Hebrew University, Professor Yo'ash Vedyah, who listened to the plan. He was so taken by it that he moved quickly to convince the board to broaden its scope, allowing Hebrew University to become the home of this new, mysterious and top secret army program. This was not the first nor the last time that an Israeli secretary knew more about making the right connections than the "experts." It seems to be built into Israeli culture.

Internal meetings following the decision at Hebrew University often descended to fighting over the content of the program and whether it would be academically rigorous enough. The university didn't want to hand out degrees to candidates they did not believe were worthy.

Several generals, including some in the general staff, wanted to kill Talpiot in its infancy. They thought it would cost far too much money, and that it was too elitist.

One of the IDF's many redeeming qualities is that it is the great equalizer in the nation. It didn't matter if you were smart or dumb, rich or poor, you were in the nation's army with people you might not ever normally come into contact. The IDF truly is an army of the people, a place where everyone is needed. The disgruntled generals felt that a program like Talpiot would turn that line of thinking on its ear, and they were vocal in their opposition.

Colonel Machnes always defended the program, "I was always straight to the point when people in the army said Talpiot wasn't necessary. I would always speak up, no matter who was on the other side. [I would] say we were important and the state needed Talpiot. I was constantly fighting with higher ranking officers in the opening years, officers who were trying to squash our budget. There were numerous arguments."

And to many generals, the thought of Talpiot becoming the army's top priority was abhorrent. They needed fighters. They needed motivated young Israelis to fly planes and drive tanks; they needed boots on the ground, and they needed to secure the nation from the sea.

Talpiot's recruiters were forced to jockey for position, smashing elbows with other officers representing other elite branches of the army. There was infighting. There was subterfuge. Bad and conflicting advice was given to potential recruits.

Fortunately, the first commander of Talpiot was an indomitable personality, Dan Sharon. His war experience had taught him that there was a need for such a program well before the idea began taking off. On the first day of fighting in the Yom Kippur War, Egyptian warplanes fired Russian-made Kelt missiles at his base. The Kelts were precursors to today's cruise missiles, boasting pinpoint accuracy. Major Sharon saw some of the reserve foot soldiers who were on his base come up with a quick way to defeat and deceive the Kelts by tapping into their Israeli radar systems that were on a similar frequency. "I thought, why are these guys here? They should be at the Ministry of Defense. At this point, I knew we were wasting resources and needed to do better."

Sharon was a long-time friend of Felix Dothan. (They used to meet on Fridays for a spot of brandy.) He was very eager to help Dothan, so when the program was finally accepted in 1978, Dothan asked him to lead Talpiot and Sharon accepted. He had just completed his PhD dissertation at Hebrew University on "the development of thinking and how one can improve his or her own thinking."

In order to take the Talpiot position, however, the army had to reactivate him. They did so immediately, with the higher rank of lieutenant colonel (*sgan aluf*, executive officer of a brigade).

Sharon looked to many places for help and advice; he'd never started a military unit before. Benny Peled, former chief of the Israeli Air Force and architect of the IAF's stunning defeat of the Egyptian and Syrian air forces in the Six-Day War, offered his services. Sharon recalls, "Peled was always very positive, but critical and cautious at the same time. He always had a very sharp mind. He said to me, 'Listen, when you construct a bridge, you always leave a weak spot where you can destroy the bridge with one single stick of dynamite, if necessary. Maybe we are making a mistake, so don't forget: in case this program is unsuccessful, you need to get out.'"

Sharon quickly discovered there would be bumps on the road, particularly in finding the super soldiers he needed for Talpiot. He discovered that he was in competition with a preexisting elite computer and communications eavesdropping unit called Unit 8200. Its recruiters were active precisely where Talpiot hoped to attract candidates.

"It became clear to us when we came to the field, the guys

from 8200 were already there, and already had recruited.... An unpleasant situation developed and I decided to solve this problem. There was a colonel in intelligence who was responsible for their training, Sasson Sahaik. At first, he didn't want to meet with me to discuss this issue, but ultimately he agreed. We sat in the Harley Café in Tel Aviv. I looked him straight in the eye, I told him this is about our existence here. Then I said, 'Tell me – is it good for us to fight? Let's compromise. We'll find them together and we'll ask each student what he wants. That's it. If you have one or two who are exactly for you, take them. But in the end, let the candidates do what they want.'" Like many things in Israel, that informal deal was sealed with a handshake, and the truce held.

In the early days, top generals also argued that army recruits shouldn't be studying in a classroom. But Colonel Machnes made sure they were fighters first. He repeatedly pointed out to Talpiot detractors that "our Talpiot recruits had Israeli Air Force uniforms and I insisted they'd be an army unit, not students in the army. I ran it as a fighting unit."

Dothan, Yatziv and Colonel Machnes set the standards for admission and recruitment very high. In one of their original organizational memos they wrote:

> We need applicants with a high IQ. We are looking for the top 5 percent when it comes to intelligence, creative ability, the ability to focus, stable and pleasant personalities; these people will need to be in constant contact with the employees of Research and Development of the Ministry of Defense, combat officers and professionals, scientists in institutions of higher education and engineers and technicians in the

institute where they'll work…. [Applicants must have] dedication to their homeland and the strong will to survive in the unit.[2]

That is clearly not an easy shopping list, especially when the new unit had to compete with Special Forces units and the Israeli Air Force, which had similar requirements. Both had two huge advantages over Talpiot. First off, every potential recruit had heard of both; and the smartest and most able students had long strived to join them. Everyone knew that the training, connections and prestige of belonging to those units would later help them in their post-army careers. Nobody had ever heard of Talpiot, not even some of the army's top officers, let alone the recruits.

Existing units had the added advantage of public image. Army service in Israel was (and is still, though to a much lesser extent) seen as a coming of age, when boys turn into men and girls become young women. Most seventeen- and eighteen-year-olds don't want to sign up to study. They want to fight. They want to impress girls with their special insignias and berets. They want to be seen as men protecting their nation. To many, sitting in a classroom is like sitting on the bench. They want to be in the game.

Yet many of the top Israeli recruits would quickly find they didn't have a choice of where they'd go anyway. Chief of Staff Eitan wanted to make Talpiot a priority, and he was going to get as many generals on board as possible to make it happen – even if the recruits had never heard of Talpiot.

A few years after the program was created, it became

---

[2] IDF Archives.

common knowledge among senior officers in the IDF that Talpiot would be given the right of first refusal regarding all enlistees in the armed forces. If you were accepted into the training program for air force pilots but Talpiot's commanders wanted you, you would go to Talpiot. You could be a fighter pilot later, but first you were going into Talpiot.

The founders were working under the theory – backed up by research – that they could only use young men (and later, women) of a young age because they believed creativity and the proclivity to believe "anything is possible" peaks in the early twenties. If the young recruits wanted to do something in the army in addition to Talpiot, that wouldn't be a problem. But Talpiot must come first.

Recruiting in those first years was rudimentary. Army human resources officers would gather data about potential candidates from other recruitment officers through a large database. But because Talpiot didn't know exactly what criteria to judge, it was not an easy process.

Talpiot recruitment officers would also go to schools, mostly in Tel Aviv, Jerusalem and Haifa, to talk to school principals and tell them a little about the program, hoping they could connect and find appropriate candidates about to graduate high school and enlist in the army. But this was far from a scientific process, and many capable students and candidates living outside of Israel's three main cities were left out of the mix. It took the IDF years to figure out how to equalize the recruiting process and cover the nation's smaller and less wealthy areas.

Still, finding the right recruits was a problem. Dothan and Yatziv began working on criteria to help them make sure the right candidates were applying and being accepted. In the early years, they wanted to isolate candidates who would be able to deal with a lot of new physics and mathematics material in a short amount of time, understand it to the degree that they could apply it to actual projects, achieve a bachelor's degree and absorb the material usually given to exceptional students in a four-year period – in just three years.

The original tests for Talpiot tested both cognitive function and creativity. (Later, a component designed to test for future success in a team environment was added.) The entry tests were devised by experts in both math and physics. In addition, psychometric tests were devised to test for intelligence, the ability to learn new subjects and, of course, personality traits.

The students taking the tests in the early years of Talpiot recruitment were often puzzled. They had never been in this position before. These were personal questions, not questions they had expected: How do you feel about yourself? How do you feel when you don't do as well as you had hoped on an assignment? Do you feel nervous when addressing a group?

After those first tests, the pool of several hundred applicants had to be whittled down to several dozen. Now things really got interesting. A few months before the enlistment date, candidates were called in for personal interviews. One by one, they were called into a room. The seventeen-year-old high school student would sit before a panel of eight to ten people, many of whom were high-ranking army officers, heads of the IDF from the Defense Ministry's Research and Development arm, MAFAT. (There will be more at the end of this chapter on MAFAT, which helps oversee Talpiot in conjunction with the Israeli Air Force. More importantly, representatives of MAFAT are later very influential in analyzing the Talpiot graduates and in aiding in their choice of where they will serve in the army after they graduate from three years of intense coursework.)

The personal interview part of the testing phase usually lasted about thirty minutes. The panel scrutinized how the candidate acted under pressure, how poised and creative he was, how he fielded questions and his ability to communicate with older, more powerful and more sophisticated men.

The interviewing committee became known as the Character Acceptance Committee. There were many levels to "the interview," but staples included asking candidates questions regarding math and physics, to find out how well the potential candidates could understand new material. In some cases, they were given material to read, then quizzed. They were asked seemingly simple questions to find out how much they enjoyed learning about science and how curious they were. Questions may have included "How does an airplane fly?" and "How does a refrigerator work?"

Haggai Scolnicov, a Talpiot graduate, reflected on the grueling test phase, particularly the committee interview. It seemed to him that they were looking for leadership and a candidate's ability to take on difficult tasks, technological leadership in effect. For instance, "They ask you to explain physical phenomena which are likely well beyond what anyone ever studied in school and to do the best you can with a question you won't know the real answer to. They want to know…can he think outside of the box? They're nice, but they're also intense about it. You know this is no joke when…you're surrounded by professors and high-ranking army officers."

In one case that has become legend, after being asked about his hobbies, a candidate spoke during his interview about his love of playing music. He compared his fascination with composing music to his love and interest in physics. He was then asked how he might use both of those interests to create the perfect sound. The young man described his guitar in great detail and then explained how he might use a series of connections to amplify the sound. After the candidate left the room, one of the commanders conducting the interview slapped himself on the head and said to the other interviewers, "I've been trying to build an electric guitar for my son. He just explained exactly what has been missing!"[3]

Another candidate's interview didn't go quite as well. The lad was asked if he was a Zionist. He answered, "I love Israel, but I will probably take what I learn in this program and apply it to professional pursuits outside of the country." That man didn't make the cut. When his father found out, he marched the boy back to some of the men on the interview committee and told them his teenager didn't know what he was talking about, and of course he was a Zionist who wanted to help his country – forever. The surprised members of the committee swore to the father they actually liked his answer. The kid had been honest. But there were other reasons, they claimed, why he wasn't accepted.

Several Talpiot graduates also said they were asked different formations of this question: "How many gas stations are there in Israel?" Most of them say they'd estimate the population, then divide it into an assumption of how many cars are on the roads in Israel and they'd try to devise some sort of logical and mathematical equation. But to a man all laughed about it later, saying they now understand "the committee" wasn't looking for an accurate answer. They simply wanted to see how potential recruits acted under stress and how they thought through problems.

[3] 30th Anniversary Talpiot Yearbook Published in Hebrew.

When a young woman going through the testing told the committee she spoke Italian, they were impressed, for Italian is not a language many Israelis learn to speak. Upon hearing this, one member of the committee asked her, "How many people have seen Michelangelo's statue 'David' in the Galleria dell'Academia in Florence?"

Another candidate who ultimately succeeded and gained acceptance to Talpiot says, "I was told, 'Give me the name of a scientist that you look up to and would like to emulate.' I thought to myself, don't pick Einstein, don't pick Einstein, don't pick Einstein…but I panicked and Einstein it was. I then proceeded to pretty much make up an answer, but the key was to sound confident and competent. They all probably laughed at me after I left the room."

Another successful candidate found the "mind games" very stressful. He had been asked, "What is a black hole and how does it work?" He recalls, "To be honest, I really thought that maybe they didn't exactly know either."

While some high school Talpiot candidates regard these psychological tests and personality profiling stimulating and others find it stressful, the personal interview, "the student versus the committee," remains an invaluable part of the testing today. It is a rite of passage and still the cornerstone of Talpiot selections.

Yet in the opening years of the program, heavy concentration on psychological stamina and academics seems to have been overplayed. Talpiot recruiters came under criticism for not finding team players.

One of the most famous Talpiot graduates is a man named Eli Mintz. He characterizes the early Talpiot people as "very strange. It was twenty eccentric nerds put together and then told by army officers – who often had no idea what we were working on, or how we were doing it – to 'get along.'"

"Getting along" proved to be a formidable challenge to many of those super-smart teens. Mintz confesses, "Like many others in the program, I had come from environments where I thought I was always the smartest. So when you're finally in a place where you think, 'Wow, I'm not the smartest guy in the room,' it was great. It was a new challenge. But not everyone was programmed to think like that, and it led to personality problems." He reflects that learning to work with others who are smarter than he was the most important thing Talpiot had taught him.

Those personality problems would soon be addressed. After a few years, Talpiot recruiters added a crucial new phase to the process. They wanted to see which candidates could work well as a group under challenging conditions. To this day, new recruits are measured in this part of the testing by former Talpiot graduates.

Specifically, these tests can consist of working with team members to come up with a proposal for as many ways to use a bicycle or a shoe they can think of. Others are asked to design something as a team. Some tests include using children's building blocks to construct something. All of this is happening under tight deadlines, sometimes in hot rooms. To add tension and pressure to the situation, former Talpiot graduates are lurking behind, recording every move and every word – or at least the candidates are made to feel like that's what's happening.

By the sixth or seventh year, recruiting became more formalized. Professors Yatziv and Dothan knew who they were looking for and how to find them. And by then there were actual Talpiot graduates with a bigger say in the program. That was so valuable because their tangible experience led to practical revisions in the Talpiot selection process.

In fact, a good number of changes took place during the early years in both the vision and development of Talpiot as its founders struggled with practical concerns and unforeseen problems. In the opening stages of Talpiot, Professors Yatziv and Dothan weren't quite sure where they wanted to take the program, according to Talpiot graduate Amir Schlachet. "They envisioned a Palo Alto Research Center, similar to the one set up and developed by Xerox. They wanted to take young people and put them in a research institute and have them think of ways to come up with new weapons, emphasizing breakthrough technologies. [Initially they intended] that graduates would stay together forever at the research center. But in the first year, Talpiot commanders realized the idea had to change because there were simply not enough resources to make it happen in a country as small as Israel. You can't just build labs and think tanks in Israel; we don't have the resources. So instead they said, 'We'll train them and send them to places where R and D infrastructure already exists, namely in the army, air force and navy, and also with Israeli defense contractors.'"

For Talpiot to work, it would take resourcefulness, dedication and the humility to revise the original plan. And none of these qualities were beyond its founders, particularly Felix Dothan, according to Amir Peleg, of the fifth Talpiot class. He describes the professor as the real driving force behind the program. "Dothan was very proud of being one of the first to say that something needs to be done to create a program like this. He was such a relaxed, nice guy. Not too dogmatic, and always genuine. He really cared about Talpiot, about the army and about Israel – and he did the best he could to turn his vision into a reality."

Professor Dothan could not have forged Talpiot without the vigorous support and cooperation of MAFAT. Because Talpiot and MAFAT are intertwined, it is important to understand the nature of this important facet of Israel's military. Early on when the state was created, Prime Minister David Ben-Gurion wanted to keep the fighting men and women separate from the men and women who would control the money and the budget. He knew the army would play a large role in the makeup and development of the nation, but he wanted to separate the guns and the money in order to maintain a balance of power, and to disable any future general from controlling both the army and the budget at the same time. In Israel, the Ministry of Defense is generally operated by civilians who control the budget for military spending, and the IDF is run by Israel's generals.

MAFAT is the Hebrew acronym for Administration for the Development of Weapons and Technological Infrastructure. The special department that was the precursor to MAFAT was just in the beginning stages of working together with Israel's defense contractors when the Yom Kippur War broke out. That new research and development department had little to do with the fighting. During those three hard weeks of war, the head of research and development, Uzi Eilam, had taken over this crucial unit only a few weeks before the fighting began, and like most Israelis, he really had no idea the war was coming. During the war, he lent out his staffers to different army units to help in any way they could, yet he retained a core research and development team in case an assignment came their way.

MAFAT was officially established in the early 1980s by Defense Minister Ariel Sharon; he envisioned it as an umbrella for all things R&D in the Israeli military. The new department also had a Foreign Relations Unit that was tasked with buying and selling weapons abroad.

MAFAT's main goal was and still is to develop the Israeli defense industry – all the Israeli contractors large and small – and get them on one page in order to work more closely with the Israeli Ministry of Defense.

When Talpiot was founded, MAFAT soon took on leadership and administration of the program. Filled with some of the brightest engineering and military management minds in all of Israel, MAFAT has the final say on who gets into the program and who doesn't. Though the air force is directly responsible for the cadets' military training on a day-to-day basis, MAFAT is involved in the education of Talpiot students every step of the way. It helps nurture Talpiot's young cadets by taking responsibility for their training and coursework.

Within the organization there is a special team known as the steering committee that drives the program from the outside. Headed by the man or woman serving as Deputy to the Chief Scientist of MAFAT, this committee meets several times a year to evaluate and tinker with Talpiot, changing or updating courses as needed. Talpiot's commanding officer and a representative of Hebrew University also sit on the steering committee. Sometimes a select number of Talpiot graduates are also invited, as well as other representatives from Israeli defense contractors or high-ranking officers in the Israeli ground forces, navy and air force. The committee is also responsible for coming up with strategies to decide where each soldier will serve after graduation.

From its inception, one of MAFAT's many missions is to supply Israel with a never-ending line of highly educated, highly motivated and like-minded soldiers who will better arm and protect Israel. Taking a vital role in the development and administration of Talpiot fulfills that mission.

CHAPTER 4

POLISHING THE PROGRAM

O ne of the many reasons for the overwhelming success of the Talpiot program is the open mindedness of the officers who run it. Yes, there's a bureaucracy. But when it counts, the army knows how to do the job right. Flexibility and tolerance for trial and error are key in honing a program that's part academic, part hard-core warrior training and partly responsible for developing weapons and intelligence tools of the future. From the start, the founders of Talpiot were men of science, and they knew that making mistakes was part of advancement. And the army was quick to realize that Talpiot's officers and soldiers needed flexibility to try new things. Sometimes they'd achieve success and sometimes they wouldn't, but it was clear nobody should fear failure. From the program's inception, Talpiot's student-soldiers were instilled with a sense that making a mistake is perfectly acceptable, as long as you learn from it. That kind of mental freedom is a prerequisite for true creativity, and creativity is the key to innovation.

As the program matured into its sixth year, it became clear that the students were sometimes more learned in some ways than their instructors and senior officers. The Ministry of Defense began looking for someone to take charge who understood the cadets better. In order to find the right person, they looked inward.

Ophir Shoham, an outstanding graduate of the second class of Talpiot, recommended to the IDF and the Ministry of Defense that a former member of Talpiot was best suited to lead it. They asked him if he had anyone in mind. He immediately recommended his friend and fellow member of Talpiot's second class, Opher Yaron.

Yaron is from Kiryat Bialik, just north of Haifa. After enlisting in Talpiot and getting his degree from Hebrew University, Yaron spent five years in Israel's communication corps, improving Israel's existing networks, making them more flexible, efficient and more secure. When asked, officials at Israel's Ministry of Defense would only say that Yaron's work was "groundbreaking...and still classified," even three decades later.

Despite the advancements in communications that Yaron had developed, he was still unsure about what his next step would be. He wanted to stay in the army and extend his time serving the country, but he was looking for a new challenge. When Shoham approached Yaron about leading Talpiot, he thought, "It's an interesting opportunity; I want to do more than just technical work. I want a chance to work with people rather than just things."

Moreover, he strongly agreed with Shoham that Talpiot would be best served by a graduate who knew the program and the capabilities of the recruits. "I felt I could relate to them.

They were very smart, very confident in themselves. They think they know everything and that their way is the right way, so it's hard for them to accept authority sometimes. I was like that at eighteen, and I'd had the same experiences. So I thought it would be good for the program for the recruits to relate to a graduate."

He took over the program in its seventh class in 1985. After studying other successful educational programs, he was inspired by American Ivy League schools that not only had great academic programs, but could also brag about their great traditions. The seventh year of a program is too early to have a true tradition, but Yaron knew that Talpiot was capable of establishing a tradition that would be the envy of other IDF units and academic programs in Israel. And fostering such tradition was crucial, he reflects, because "the early excitement for the program was starting to wear off. There was a leveling off of resources for Talpiot. When I came in, I wanted to reinvigorate the program to create a new tradition where it would be known as a unit and a part of the army that was constantly innovating."

Yaron didn't want to make immediate and dramatic changes for the sake of making change. He believes that's often a mistake made by new chief executives in the business world. Instead, he wanted to build on what had already been established and enhance it.

In the year before Yaron arrived, Talpiot had started recruiting women. Six females were drafted in 1984, none in 1985 and three in the eighth class. As commander of Talpiot, Yaron never tried to recruit women differently from the way he recruited young men. "We simply sought the best people." The women who were recruited wanted the full program, though typically high school girls do not want to commit to the army for ten years. "We quickly found out it was not a problem for the women we were considering," he recalls.

For most basic training programs in the Israeli army, men and women are separated, as they're usually in single-sex units. But in Talpiot, the men and women in the same class go through drills equally and together. That means long runs and difficult hikes, shooting courses, parachuting school, obstacle courses and beyond.

Marina Gandlin (twenty-sixth class of Talpiot) admits, "I was mostly nervous about boot camp. But I talked myself into it saying to myself if other girls can do it, I can. Talpiot is a long program, of course, and a lot of people don't make it all the way through. I wasn't sure if I was going to be able to make it until I was in for six or eight months. By that time, I had built up enough confidence. Thirteen students dropped out of my class. These were people who were quite capable of doing advanced physics, but Talpiot was just too difficult for them."

With Talpiot's high drop-out rate, keeping female recruits was especially hard. Yaron recalls that with one undecided female recruit, "I wanted her to join, but I tried not to pressure. She did join. She was the lone woman in the class and wound up dropping out. I felt very bad about it."

He remained the leader of Talpiot for two years before handing over the reins to another graduate. In fact, from the time Yaron took over – with one exception, for a short period of time – only Talpiot graduates have led the program since. His bold move in accepting the job set an enduring precedent.

Two of the program's most innovative Talpiot commanders were Lieutenant Colonel Avi Poleg, Yaron's direct successor, and Major Amir Schlachet (a man who would later go on to major success at Israel's largest bank, Bank Hapoalim).

Poleg grew up in Haifa in the 1970s. As a teenager, he was quiet, curious and studious. He was also a musical prodigy, a cellist. Once a week he'd commute two hours to Tel Aviv for cello lessons. He clearly remembers the trauma of the Yom Kippur War and always wanted to help his country. But because of a few health problems, he knew he'd never be able to serve in a combat role.

When he was asked to apply for Talpiot in 1981, he had never heard of it before, like most of the enlistees of those years. The program hadn't been publicized for it was regarded as a military secret. In Israel, military secrets are closely guarded, even in families and circles of friendships; people simply know not to ask too many questions. Since nobody had yet graduated from the program in early 1981, there was nobody to ask about what happens inside of it. He had to trust his gut.

He became a member of the third class of Talpiot and never looked back. After graduating from Talpiot's academic program, he was picked by the navy to develop electro-optics for ships, first working on devices designed to deceive enemy radar and missiles, then on developing infrared and thermal cameras to detect ships, weapons, missiles and any other kind of imaginable threat.

A decade after enlisting in Talpiot, Poleg became its leader, in charge of day-to-day operations. His fieldwork in the navy helped him get to this position, one he had coveted for some time. A former superior at the Ministry of Defense said of him: "It was really perfect for Avi. First off, he's a sincere patriot. He also has a real understanding of physics. And perhaps, most important was his interest in the field of education."

During the nineties, Israel's military technology was moving forward at a rapid pace and Talpiot students and graduates were playing an outsized role in developing those technologies. Many of them, including cellular phone technology and data encryption, would soon have major civilian uses.

As the army's needs were changing, Talpiot's officers had to make adjustments to the list of desirable qualities in candidates. Teamwork was becoming a bigger part of the equation because different kinds of systems had to be integrated into different units. Each year, picking the right twenty or twenty-five people was becoming more and more important.

"Suddenly, we had to start looking for a new combination of attributes," Poleg said. In addition to high cognitive scores and scientific thinking, they were looking for people who could lead: officer testing and personality exams became crucial. Poleg revamped two parts of the exam – the group test and the interview.

"I wanted to check motivation, moral value and, of course, personality. We would run intense social simulations in which the candidate was put into a high-pressure leadership position. How do you try to motivate your classmates who might be falling behind? How do you deal with those who refuse to take part in a certain project or activity? My goal here was to see how candidates coped with social issues, leadership issues and paying attention to everyone. I needed to be confident that the candidates I picked would be creative, intelligent, inventive, with the ability to move from one area to another, and be able to take leadership in a group while being part of that group. It was also critical to get a sense of how cadets might act when having to deal with someone above them and below them. Finally, I also needed a sense of their moral values and willingness to make a contribution to their country and society. I was always confident I could move the right students forward, but they had to have the roots. The trick was distinguishing who did and who didn't."

In the committee interview, Poleg might say, "Tell me something interesting that you saw last month that you didn't know, what you learned about it and how you increased your knowledge. Maybe an interesting instrument, an interesting science program you watched on television, an interesting article you read about science." This was the starting point, and he would use it to find out the level of the candidate's curiosity and how far he'd go to satisfy that curiosity. "I was looking to see if the candidate made a real effort to investigate."

Poleg also refined the process of assessing the candidate's ability to think. Famously, he would give them a sophisticated article from a science journal about something he was confident the recruit didn't understand and had not studied. The recruit would quickly read the article and then was asked a series of questions about it. The goal was not to test him on his knowledge, but to observe his thinking process.

Poleg believed that an incisive committee interview gave him the best sense of the candidate, well beyond test scores. In one memorable instance, a candidate had not done particularly well on the previous testing, but Poleg gave him a simulation. "He started to flourish...he was so enthusiastic and really animated. 'I would do this and I would do that...' It was as if he were suddenly conducting an orchestra; as if he had found his voice right then and there in front of the committee. This was exactly the answer I was looking for. He has it! I viewed the committee in part as a trainer to pull something out of a candidate, and I used similar methods as a commander and educator once those potential recruits were in the program."

Of course, there is no foolproof way of picking the best

cadets for Talpiot. As Poleg had projected, social testing took on increased importance in the late 1990s and earliest years of the twenty-first century.

It is generally accepted that no Talpiot commander should stay in the same position for too long. By 2003, the timing was perfect for new ideas and new leadership, and Amir Schlachet became commander of Talpiot.

By the time Schlachet was planning his army career at the age of sixteen, the veil of secrecy over Talpiot was starting to lift and the program had become known throughout the country. Soon it became a top priority for any young Israeli who was interested in physics, science and math and was able to achieve a high academic status. In many ways, students who target admission to Talpiot are akin to students in the United States who want to go to Harvard, MIT, Princeton or Yale.

At the age of seventeen, joining Talpiot wasn't exactly Schlachet's life goal. But as he made it further and further through the labyrinth of exams, he became more and more interested and more hopeful that he'd make the cut. "I knew I wanted to do cool stuff; I knew engineers and physicists. I didn't really know what research and development was, but I liked the idea of merging science and defense."

After his three years of course work, he graduated with his degree in science and physics from Hebrew University. He was placed in an air force research and development unit by the Talpiot commanders and Ministry of Defense, and worked in a special unit developing airborne electronic systems (used in communications, radar and air-to-air and air-to-ground targeting).

As he was finishing his Talpiot service, he was ready to pursue an advanced degree and then move to the world of business. But an Israeli Ministry of Defense legend (and Talpiot graduate), Eviatar Matania, a man who would later be known as "the right hand of Talpiot," asked Schlachet to stay. Matania recognized something extra special in Amir Schlachet: he saw a man who understood the need for Israel to be ahead of the curve in technology, a great project manager and an officer who could get everyone together to push toward a common goal. Matania offered him the chance to command the entire day-to-day program and to revitalize it.

Schlachet immediately accepted and put his business career on hold, indefinitely. With ruthless honesty, he assessed every feature of Talpiot, "looking at the entire program from above. If something added value, we wanted to strengthen it. If it was weak, we wanted to drop it. We changed the software for aggregate numbers-crunching. Talpiot keeps evolving and to a large extent; so does the screening process. One of Talpiot's biggest strengths is that we do our own screening, so we wanted to improve and intensify that. We redesigned the entire process. We are never on lock down and that's a tremendous strength."

Breathing new life into the program, Schlachet upgraded the position of top officer to a Talpiot graduate and gave him more responsibility – he stays for a few years, not just one year, before moving on to something or shipping out from the army. "We didn't want to invest extra training in future leaders and then have them leave after just one year," Schlachet explains.

While still heading Talpiot, Schlachet persuaded a former class commander to stay after his time in the army was up. Dror Ben Eliezer was given a three-year role as head of admissions under Schlachet. Dror is one of the few Talpiot graduates who also had a brother in the program, Barak. They had grown up inside the Old City walls of Jerusalem, playing American football with yeshivah students from the United States. Barak would later use many of the management techniques he learned in Talpiot and apply them to Israel's police force.

Schlachet is a very humble man, as are most Talpiot graduates. He begrudgingly admits that colleagues and other Talpiot graduates might be right when they said, "Amir breathed new life into the program, revamped it and made it better." What he is most proud of is that he revolutionized the screening process, which was in a transitional phase at the time. As the testing tilted increasingly toward social and personality factors, he actually came up with a better way to find out who is right and who is not right for the program. The "quiet tests" (where candidates don't know what they're being tested for, or that they're being tested at all) reveal a good deal, thanks to psychometric advisors. These are third-year Talpiot students, (chosen on the basis of commanders' recommendations) and Talpiot graduates who have gone through special certification to participate.

Marina Gandlin became a proctor for the social tests given to prospective Talpiot cadets. She describes the group tests that are given over two days. "We split them into teams and ask them to build something out of paper or out of blocks, to see how they interact with other people. I don't want someone telling the other people what to do and what not to do. I don't want people who are rude or too pushy. No violence and no shouting. Those are definitely signs you're not right for Talpiot. I know it sounds funny, but you can easily tell who's good and comfortable and who has ideas about how to get the project completed, and also who can get others on his or her side to complete that project. We watch them move forward with their projects right in front of them. There are no two-way mirrors or anything like that, just ten or twelve people in a room working, and two or three Talpiot graduates watching them to see how they behave."

When asked what makes Talpiot so unique when compared with engineering or physics programs in other armies, Schlachet gives three reasons: 1) the fine-tuned selection process; 2) unique training, both academic and military, with emphasis on the big picture; and 3) success in finding the right position for the graduate to serve.

This last factor is critical, both to the Talpiot graduate and to the country. Talpiot officers work to build job descriptions for positions in research and development that are high on the priority lists of the army, navy and air force. "We want them to be interested in the things they'll be doing after graduation," says Schlachet, "because, hopefully, they'll be doing those jobs for at least five years. If they're interested, they'll be even more motivated. The solutions we're working on for the IDF aren't trivial, for some the work will be the difference between life and death. We work on placement of each graduate during their entire three years of study. Our goal is to put each Talpiot graduate in a position where he or she will have maximum impact."

Schlachet points out that one of the strengths of the Talpiot experience is that it is collaborative. "Somehow, it is not competitive in any way. In fact it is one of the least competitive places I've ever worked in. People help others even if it means they get a lower grade or do less on something. It's fantastic. Very close ties are built, maintained and kept forever."

Despite the fact that Talpiot graduates have taken responsibility of day-to-day operations of the program, there are still people above them from Israel's Ministry of Defense, particularly insiders at MAFAT, the Israel Defense Force's research and development arm. Throughout the selection process, administration of the program and placement of graduates, these career army officers make sure Talpiot gets what it needs and that Talpiot gives back what the army needs from them.

A high-ranking member of the Israeli Ministry of Defense (who would not allow his name to be used) pointed out that "the unique thing about Talpiot is that it continues to reinvent itself, stay ahead of the times and improve itself. Part of that is because the graduates care so much; and they're somehow constantly able to leave something better behind. It would be great if the rest of the country were like that as well!"

CHAPTER 5

IT ALL STARTS IN HIGH SCHOOL

O nce the Talpiot program got off the ground and had refined its selection procedures, it began to make a name for itself as an elite unit. Today, thirty-six years after the program began, the IDF's website describes the exclusivity of Talpiot: "The program accepts 50 outstanding students from those in the science tracks in high schools." Competition for admission to the program is fierce.

Ron Berman is an uber-student who not only was accepted to Talpiot's nineteenth class, but also has been educated in Denmark, Tel Aviv University, the University of Pennsylvania's Wharton School, and is currently studying for his PhD at the University of California, Berkeley. This student of students advises anyone trying to get into Talpiot: "It all starts in high school."

Many of Israel's high schools are actually dedicated to helping their students get into elite technology and "thinking" units like Talpiot. One initiative in Jerusalem was designed

specifically with Talpiot in mind. The Israel Center for
Excellence through Education is run by former Talpiot
commander Avi Poleg. He uses many of the techniques he
perfected at Talpiot and shares them with schools run by the
state, throughout Israel. The Center is integral in setting the
curriculum and helping to run one of the few boarding schools
in the State of Israel, the Israel Arts and Science Academy. The
school shares its campus with The Center.

Students admitted to this elite program are already extremely
talented. But the school is designed to help them focus on
mathematics, chemistry, physics and computer science at a
higher level than they could get at a state-run school anywhere
else in Israel. Some students commute from the Jerusalem
area, but most live, sleep and eat in dorms. The teenagers at the
school come from more than a hundred diverse communities
in Israel. They come from large cities and small towns, from
kibbutzim and agricultural communities, and the program is
open to both Israeli Jews and Arabs.

The Israel Arts and Science Academy and The Israel Center
for Excellence Through Education give students the tools
they need to learn better and faster, just like Talpiot cadets.
Poleg's teaching methods are the same as they were in Talpiot.
"We don't direct students to a certain point; we want to prep
them with the abilities and values and talent to cope later
on with challenges. Talpiot's philosophy of how to promote
independent thinking, curiosity and motivation is relevant
here."

When asked, "How do you implant curiosity and a
desire to learn in a student?" Poleg answers: "You're asking
for the whole Torah on one leg, as Rabbi Hillel once said."
[The famous sage was once asked if he could summarize the

entire Torah while the questioner "stands on one leg."] "In a nutshell, it is developing study units that will pull students into an adventure. We don't start by saying today we are going to learn about this or that. We start with a legend or story. We try to put the student in a position that simulates the situation. We tell them, 'This time you'll be a historian; a scientist; a detective.' Students should learn under different hats to keep it interesting. It is a way to build tasks in a moderate way, putting much of the responsibility in the hands of the students themselves. The teachers are not supposed to be the source of knowledge but rather facilitators of the learning process. That means they are there to guide the process and instruct slightly, to let the students come up with their own conclusions; to let them fail and not correct them too early. The teachers should ask many questions, but provide few answers. Answers should come from the students."

There are clear differences between a boarding school and a military base. While the end goal is the same, implementation isn't identical. But Talpiot rules and methods do hold true. Poleg sees it as his responsibility to "strengthen independent abilities and self-esteem. I deeply believe that once you teach a learner you will harvest the results later on."

Some might call the Israel Arts and Science Academy a "prep school for Talpiot." Admission to Talpiot is always in the minds of the program's students and teachers, and they've sent more than their fair share on to Talpiot success.

Nachshon, a similar program for high school students, later became prominent. It was founded by Eviatar Matania of Talpiot's sixth class. The program is named for the valiant biblical figure Nachshon ben Aminadav, the first Israelite to jump into the Red Sea before the waters parted. While

Nachshon's students are not necessarily Talpiot candidates, several cadets have come from the prestigious program.

In Israel, many of the top high schools align themselves with top universities, either formally or informally. One of Talpiot's earliest "feeder high schools" was a school called Handassa'eem. *Handassa* means engineering and geometry in Hebrew. It used to be closely affiliated with Tel Aviv University and has sent Talpiot some of its finest graduates, including Eli Mintz. He recalls, "I was recruited to Talpiot after the army received a recommendation from the principal of my high school at Handassa'eem. Five people from my high school class went on to Talpiot. Overall, Handassa'eem has sent a high percentage."

Another prominent graduate who went on to Talpiot is Ophir Kra-Oz. The principal at the time was Yohannan Eilat, who "turned it into a tech powerhouse. He used to take a map of Silicon Valley and put it over Haifa and tell everyone, 'look – a perfect fit.' That was in 1988, long before Silicon Valley was something everybody in the world knew about. He was a real visionary."

While Kra-Oz was in high school, he and many other future Talpiot students were so far ahead of their instructors in computer science, they wound up teaching the classes. As the world adapted to computer-based life, teachers had trouble keeping up at first. It quickly became clear the tide was changing throughout the globe as students began teaching the teachers.

Yet a big advantage emerged at Handassa'eem in those years. Many Russian immigrants with very sophisticated education couldn't find work at their level in Israel; and so, many became teachers at Handassa'eem.

The school has since moved and now stands in the town of Herzliyah, just north of Tel Aviv. The principal today is Orit Rozen. Handassa'eem furnishes so many recruits to top army technological units "because of the multitude of projects the school offers, which is unprecedented in the country and abroad. There is a diversity and high level of scientific work, including a combination of various disciplines – computer science, technology, medical science and more." Today "more" includes robotics and facilities for students showing an early acumen for satellites, aerospace and bio-technology.

In Haifa, not far from the Technion, is a high school named Leo Baeck. Students are accepted from all walks of Israeli life. Many pay some tuition, though about 10 percent are on full scholarship. There are forms of assistance for other students as well.

The mission of the school is to provide a pluralistic education for its students who come to the school from all over the northern half of the country. There are about a thousand students and 150 teachers, a ratio just about any school in the world would envy. Leo Baeck set a modern-day record in 2005 by sending five graduates to Talpiot including Marina Gandlin, who later became an early pioneer in short-range missile defense and the Iron Dome.

In Jerusalem, a prestigious public high school also known for supplying Talpiot with numerous cadets is known simply as L'yada, which translates to "next to" in English. It gets its name from being "next to" Hebrew University.

Israel is a country where kids have to grow up fast so they can contribute to the security and well-being of the state early on. And the Israeli high school system is actually so important that it has become a major source of fundraising overseas through programs like "Friends of Israel Sci-Tech Schools." Seventy-three high schools fit into this special category, where the focus is on robotics, engineering, nanotechnology, bio-medical engineering, aerospace and computer science. These schools have not only educated scores of Talpiot cadets, hundreds of their other graduates have gone on to provide important security solutions and become Israel's high-tech business leaders.

A strong spirit of giving back permeates Israeli society. Many executives who have attained the highest levels of Israel's corporate hierarchy have established ways of helping the country, its students and future leaders. Former Israeli President Shimon Peres has initiated one such project. Over the last several years, the popular statesman has been helping Israeli high-tech CEOs meet and mentor the nation's most promising high school students through a program he helped found with the charitable organization, the Rashi Foundation (designed to encourage Israel's teenage inventors). He has enlisted the help and support of many of Israel's biggest corporate leaders, including Sammy Segol who runs Keter Plastic, one of Israel's biggest companies and biggest exporters. Segol encourages his employees to get involved in mentoring future leaders as well.

One of those employees is Barak Ben-Eliezer, a man who could not possibly be more focused on bettering the state of Israel. (Selected for the Talpiot program in 1992, he was part of the famous fourteenth class whose members founded the storage company XIV and sold it to IBM for $300 million.) Two of Ben-Eliezer's Talpiot connections have also dedicated a good part of their time to helping young, enterprising minds. Uri Rokni develops algorithms for an Israeli company called Mobileye. (He's working on greatly improving the safety of driving by putting high-tech anti-crash systems in the cars we drive. The company listed on the Nasdaq Stock Market in August 2014 and the stock quickly soared, becoming the darling of Wall Street.) In his spare time, he volunteers to help increase the level of competency in math in Israel's high schools.

Uri Barenholz graduated with Ben-Eliezer's fourteenth class of Talpiot. He went from data storage to biological engineering research at the world renowned Weizmann Institute in Rehovot, Israel. For fun, he teaches physics at a junior high school in Holon, a suburb of Tel Aviv.

Some of the students he teaches, like the talented young scientists being graduated from specialized high schools, will set their sights on advanced university degrees. Many will aim for admission to Talpiot, for they know that it is the stepping-stone to the best university education, the highest army accolades and a promising future.

CHAPTER 6

THE WORLD'S FASTEST LEARNING CURVE

From the start, the Israeli army and founders of Talpiot knew that they'd need to outsource some of the educational aspects of the program to Hebrew University.

Most Israelis don't start at universities until they are at least twenty-two years old, four or five years later than most students in the United States. Most Israelis are discharged from regular army duty and then go to see the world. They go to India. They trek through Nepal. They escape to Thailand. In fact, there are so many Israelis in parts of those countries, street signs, store and hotel markers are in Hebrew. One shopkeeper in India was shocked to find out there were only about six and a half million Israelis. He thought that since his town was constantly overrun with men and women from the Jewish state, there must be hundreds of millions of them. Other young Israelis go to South America for months at a time, hiking through the Andes. Many go to both Asia and South America.

When they return to Israel, they may register in one of Israel's nine universities, many of which are world renowned, including Tel Aviv University, Ben-Gurion University of the Negev, the Technion in Haifa, and, of course, Jerusalem's Hebrew University. Others might go to one of several dozen colleges in Israel.

But because Talpiot cadets serve at least nine years in the military, they immediately begin studying for their academic degrees at the age of eighteen, when they enlist. When they finish their coursework at Hebrew University, they have their bachelor's degree in mathematics, physics and/or computer science. This advantage gives them peace of mind, knowing that they won't have to start their studies after they're out of the military.

When the army is paying for you to study, however, you don't have the luxury of falling behind. In Talpiot, if you do drop back, you'll get kicked out.

Speed has always been an important part of the program. Because Talpiot students get fewer weeks to study than their university counterparts, the academic program moves faster. One reason for that is simply because the cadets are in the army and they have other things to do. Another reason is that the army is intentionally training the cadets in how to think faster.

There is no magic to making a student learn faster. The way it is done is to emphasize group learning. The thinking is that if you're with other cadets in a military-like setting twenty-four hours a day, seven days a week, you bond. When part of the group moves faster, the rest of the group will keep the pace.

The speed of the coursework is much quicker than at a regular university. The cadets train and learn as a class.

Academic competition is not part of the program and there is
no cheating in Talpiot. Many of the professors allow students to
share work, as they encourage cadets to help one another. The
thinking is that as each cadet brings different kinds of strengths
from different backgrounds, integration is greatly encouraged.
That emphasis on teamwork helps create high levels and higher
speeds for development and for learning the course materials.

But sometimes that speed can be a problem and the 25
percent dropout rate attests to the challenge. Even some of
the top Talpiot recruits who went on to become some of the
most successful Israelis of all time have complained Talpiot's
coursework moves too fast.

Marius Nacht is a co-founder of Israel-based Check Point
Software Technologies. Their Internet protection software
defends almost all of the companies in the Fortune 500 from
web-based attacks. Nacht is a graduate of the second class of
Talpiot. He was born in Romania while his parents waited
anxiously for the Romanian government to grant their family
exit visas. In the 1960s, Romania held its Jewish citizens
hostage. If they wanted to leave, the Jewish Federation of
North America had to cough up a $5,000 ransom for every exit
visa. His parents had started the immigration process a decade
before the paperwork finally came through.

Nacht was three years old at the time, and does not recall
his first days in Israel. But he does remember growing up in
a rough, industrialized part of the coastal town of Ashkelon.
He says his family's situation gradually improved to the point
where they were eking out a middle-class existence. Back
then, standardized testing wasn't exactly part of the norm, so
Nacht's family didn't realize Marius had a special academic
gift – and neither did Marius.

His father insisted that he attend a vocational high school, a place where he could learn a trade. Marius attended ORT, one of many programs funded by the global Jewish community. He says, "I wasn't interested in it. I was doing what he told me to do. We studied many things, including electronics."

In 1980 an army recruiter came around looking for the brightest students. It was rare for the army to look beyond the established high schools in the major population centers of Jerusalem, Tel Aviv and Haifa. And it was even rarer, in those early days, for the Talpiot program to recruit someone from outside of those areas. But from Marius's class, two students were selected for Talpiot testing.

Marius was intrigued by the exams. Acceptance in Talpiot meant more to him than just the opportunity to be part of this new and exciting part of the Israeli army. It meant he had been absorbed by the country he moved to as a boy; that his intellect had been recognized, though he came from the depressed town of Ashkelon, a town often ignored by Israel's established elite in Jerusalem, Tel Aviv and Haifa.

But once he was in the program, he wanted out. "The other guys were very, very smart in terms of math and physics, and I was not at the top of the class as I had been in high school. And it was more competitive than I expected. The five top guys would elbow the others. 'Come on, why are you asking that stupid question? The professor just said it five minutes ago, why are you asking again?' We knew that the first class, the year before ours, started with thirty students, but a year later only twenty were left. So I was sure I was going to be kicked out. I finished the first term with a lousy academic average of 65. To me it was evidence that I should drop out – and I wanted to. Why continue? I was just prolonging my military service instead of doing the things I really wanted to do.

"So I went to Hanoch Tzadik, the guy that you have to talk to if you want to leave the program. He was a psychologist. I explained to him that I'm not that good. I was getting a lot of homework and not even getting half of it done by one in the morning." Tzadik (who later became one of Israel's best known professors of psychology and a motivational coach to executives) convinced him not to quit. He told Nacht he had put a lot of tension and pressure on himself and that's why he couldn't concentrate. He made him promise that every other day he would run around the campus, five or six miles, a minimum of three times a week. Nacht recalls, "Because I was much cooler about it and not pressing myself, my average grades jumped from 65 to 85. I figured if that's the trend, I might even finish with a reasonable average – and I stayed on. Hanoch Tzadik was a very important person in my life and obviously made a huge impact."

Tzadik is an appropriate name for a psychologist who helped so many people that would later become crucial to Israel's security. The word *tzadik* in Hebrew means "righteous." It is often a title sometimes given to biblical figures. In short, a *tzadik* is someone who lives by his faith.

Hanoch Tzadik notes that for most of the Talpiot students, it was the first time in their lives they needed help and to some it was a real crisis. "Their main problem was dealing with difficulty, not the course work."

"It was my main job to help them," he affirms, but there was no blanket-solution for each cadet with a problem. "I didn't really tell them anything at first, I just listened to them. I had to make them believe they will overcome the problems, and it's a very personal thing. I really believed that most of them could overcome it. The ones that left generally did very well later, but it wasn't the right time for them. These were not failures. They just weren't ready for this kind of thing. "

Getting through Talpiot was never easy, even for those who thrived on the challenge. One such person is Doctor Aviv Tuttnauer, one of a few Talpiot graduates to go to medical school after finishing his army service. He's an anesthesiologist specializing in pediatric surgery, and he agreed to be interviewed on a busy day of surgery. We meet in the hospital lobby at Hadassah Medical Center and we talk in the locker room as he puts on his operating room scrubs. So that he'd never forget it, Tuttnauer sets his locker combination to the number representing a certain isotope of uranium that can sustain a fission chain reaction. (For him, that's a memorable figure!)

He explains what would happen during surgery, the goal of the operation and his role. The surgery will be on a two-year-old boy who has an artificial heart valve needing repair. It will be Dr. Tuttnaeur's job to sedate the child.

Around us, doctors are listening to our interview. The cardiothoracic surgeon stops his pre-operation procedures for a moment and looks at Doctor Tuttnauer. He asks in Hebrew, "Who is the person doing the interview and what's it for?" Tuttnauer replies, "It has to do with my Talpiot experience." The surgeon asks in alarm, "Isn't that all top secret?" Tuttnauer chuckles and the interview continues.

He tells me that in addition to going through the program, he also served as a commander of the fifteenth class of Talpiot. He didn't quite realize it when he was a cadet – but it hit him as a commander – that educating recruits straight out of high school has advantages. "At that age, you're not responsible for a family; no kids, no jobs. You can study until one or two in the morning if need be, and it often is need be. The army gets a class of students who are free and able to learn."

The other side of the coin is that, as youngsters, they have constant complaints. As a cadet, Tuttnauer complained about the same things he'd later have to address as a commander. "We complained that the lecturers go too fast, and it's unfair because we are tested on more than our counterparts in the university. We cover 30 percent more. And the response was always that the lecturer will go as fast as his class allows him; if you understand everything, he will go on. We would complain pretty freely about things. We were very cynical."

Before the sixth Talpiot class, the commanders of the program had not graduated from the program and they weren't completely in tune with this new breed of intellectual super soldier. But even once the commanders starting coming from the Talpiot ranks, as Tuttnauer did, there was still tension between adolescent and adult, student and teacher. "As a commander, I had difficult moments with my cadets, but it was much easier for me than for previous commanders. You simply understand the dynamics because you witnessed them. They would complain daily, weekly, about the classes, the learning materials, the extra-curricular plan, the quality of food, quality of rooms, the cleanliness of rooms, the burden of guarding the building, flaws in building security – whatever, you name it. As a commander, you know there are recurring themes. That's the way it is; that's the way it's always been."

The cadets would ask whiny questions like any other teenager. "Why are we guarding the building?" Tuttnauer would answer dully, "Because we are soldiers and that's what soldiers do. You're given two hours a week of guard duty. That doesn't hamper your studying. The issue is closed."

As we finish speaking, Tuttnauer washes, disinfects, then strides into the operating room. A small patient whose life lies in his hands is waiting.

The doctor's description of the Talpiot training reflects the goals set for each of the three years of the program. Would you be able to handle the rigors of Talpiot? Here are the expectations Talpiot has for its cadets:

First Year. Goal: Build foundations for resolving problems by learning advanced mathematics, physics and computer science.

- Basic training period of eleven to twelve weeks, followed by two semesters of studies lasting up to thirty-four weeks.
- Five to six additional weeks of military orientation, visiting the different units and branches of the IDF.
- Completion of an officer training course.

Second Year. Goal: Reach a high level of aptitude in math, physics and computer science. (Almost a third of Talpiot graduates earn a degree in computer science.)

- Thirty-six weeks of studies.
- Up to three months visiting various branches of the IDF to learn more about their problems and their need for solutions.
- Rigorous paratrooper training.

Third Year. Goal: Bring all education and training together; sharpen leadership and academic skills. This includes a broad range of courses in the sciences including electronics, aerodynamics and system authentication, as well as military technology.

- Acquire a solid background in military engineering, radar, antennas and military communication.
- Take broader range humanities and social science classes at Hebrew University, including history, art history, philosophy, Jewish thought and Arabic studies.
- Decide on a discipline and an expertise.
- Interview and audition for posts within the Israel Defense Forces.

"The project" spans all three years of Talpiot training. A few times a year, they're asked to develop and then present a project that solves a problem in the national defense spectrum. In essence, it's a warm-up exercise, designed to teach them all of the rigors and stages they will later encounter when trying to solve real-life defense dilemmas.

For "the project" they come up with an idea that solves a defense problem, create a budget for it and then produce it. They present their problem and the way they've solved it to a group of army officers who are brought in to judge and discuss the projects. On several occasions, officers have been impressed enough with a certain project that they decided to actually develop it. In addition, sometimes producing a project leads to a post-army appointment for a Talpiot graduate.

Over the years, it's become commonplace for second-year students to introduce themselves to the IDF's top brass by working on these problems and the solutions. Past projects, which will be discussed later, include an early mock-up of the Iron Dome short-range missile defense shield that has been remarkably effective in knocking missiles out of the air before they reach their targets inside Israel. Another innovation, the Trophy – a tank-mounted device that automatically fires at an incoming projectile in order to protect the crew inside – had its origins in the Talpiot program.

All Talpiot classes are assigned advisors to help them through the program from beginning to end. It is the advisor's duty to serve as a contact person and liaison between the students, the army and the university professors. At the beginning of the program, founder Felix Dothan served as an advisor, a role later carried on by various professors at Hebrew University. The heads of Hebrew University's mathematics, physics and computer science programs also take on outsized roles in advising the cadets and serve as a go-between with the army. Hebrew University deans and rectors have also been integral in the program from its onset. When those three years come to an end, the cadet gets a promotion as well as that coveted degree in physics, math, computer science or all three. After graduating, most Talpiots will then continue their formal education. Many continue to study at Hebrew University while doing their army service over the next six years. The Weizmann Institute of Science is another popular destination. Talpiots who are accepted there often study for masters or doctorate degrees in biology and complex physics. On one floor of Weizmann, Talpiot students have taken over a line of offices where they are studying and experimenting with biotechnology, genetics and bio-pharm. A third choice for many Talpiot students is Tel Aviv University, where they study advanced engineering and business administration.

The Israeli army has always prided itself on being an equal opportunity employer for men and women. As noted in an earlier chapter, Talpiot was a rare exception when the program began and women were not recruited for the first several years. But by the time the twenty-fourth class was assembled in

2003, the evidence was clear – the women had arrived and had fully integrated themselves in Israel's most prestigious military program. Eleven young women were accepted into the program that year. There even have been several Talpiot marriages. *Mazal tov!*

CHAPTER 7

TRAINING TO THINK FAR BEYOND THE BOX

M atan Arazi's father was an Israeli diplomat and Matan lived for part of his youth in Japan. He was closely connected with other westerners who attended "The American School in Japan" in the 1980s.

At this time, many of the fathers of the students who attended "The American School" worked for the big American banks and brokerage firms in Tokyo. Word got around that Matan was a computer whiz. One day, he got a call from the father of one of his friends who worked for Morgan Stanley. He needed help coming up with a system that could transfer funds and stock orders quickly across phone lines. Matan, using secure communication lines provided by Morgan Stanley, was able to develop a software program that could transfer money and stock transactions instantly across the world to other Morgan Stanley offices. Now every brokerage firm in the Western world has that technology, but Matan was about fifteen years ahead of the rest of the world. He was just fourteen years old at the time. He went on to do consulting work for Goldman Sachs in Tokyo.

Back in Israel, the army realized that Matan had an enormous amount of experience working in fields needed by the military. Talpiot was quick to accept him and train him further for the army's use.

"The most amazing thing about Talpiot," says Matan, "is that the tools you learn to use can really help you make a 1 percent difference in the battlefield. Think about that. A 1 percent difference. An infantry man can't make a 1 percent difference. Maybe a pilot in a small engagement concerning a major target can make that kind of difference, but Talpiots are doing it constantly, day by day, on many different projects. In many ways, we can be the difference between life and death for hundreds, or even thousands, of people."

To make a contribution like that, you first have to be confident that you can – and that it's a possible thing to do, even if certain tasks seem impossible. "You can do anything" is instilled in Talpiot recruits. "And if you can't do it," chuckles Matan, "you know that another Talpiot graduate either has, or is on the verge of doing it. Nothing is impossible."

Talpiots are taught from the first day of induction that they can do anything they put their minds to. How does the program inject the cadets with such confidence?

Ra'anan Gefen was an early Talpiot graduate from the third class, inducted into the IDF in 1981. "Talpiot instills you with a confidence you won't find anywhere else, but you still have to define yourself," he says. "Part of that is through actual fieldwork, but the building blocks are being laid when you're doing difficult, but important, course work. Even if you don't understand it immediately, the material is taught in a practical manner, allowing even the trailers to understand it – maybe a little later, but regardless, they get it, and that gives you a high level of confidence."

Graduates are sometimes given multi-million-dollar budgets in the first months of their research and development tours of duty to create and improve the IDF's weapons arsenal. This vast amount of responsibility, and the help they're given from more experienced designers and programmers, often puts them in a position where they'll have at least some success. And the more success they have, the more they believe in themselves. They're also taught from day one that if they don't have the answer, being in Talpiot gives them a rare advantage. They will be within one or two degrees of finding another Talpiot graduate that does know the answer to the problem they're working on, or at least has answers that could lead to a solution.

Talpiot was not meant to be a machine that churns out like-minded thinkers. The founders envisioned a program that would give their cadets a foundation to do whatever they wanted to do. The program was designed to breed creativity, not conformity. And no two Talpiots come out of the program the same. The program has a life-long influence on the graduates who have gone on to do many different, but equally mind-boggling things.

Talpiot is also geared to help force recruits to work and think both within a system and outside of that system. It also strives to provide cadets with the ability to lead as many graduates will be managing and working closely with some of Israel's most inventive engineers, avionics experts, computer programmers and intelligence analysts.

One way of training a student to think is to play against his strengths, says one insider. "Don't let him rely on methods of learning or problem solving he's already used to. If you force that person to learn a different way, you're forcing him to think a different way."

Tools used to find a student's hidden potential include an overload of training, forcing students to work and study together, and pairing Talpiots with current and former class commanders. Other key factors in the future success of its graduates (in and out of the Israeli military industrial complex) are informal instruction in time management and Talpiot's proficiency in developing the student's ability to distinguish what's important from what isn't to achieve a given objective.

Talpiots are given access to something most soldiers don't have until they're older and more experienced: information about how things work. In the broader military, a soldier is a soldier, and he operates in a need-to-know environment. The goal of Talpiot is to expand students' knowledge so they're more in the loop about what happens behind that green curtain separating commanders from the men and women who rank below them.

The refining of that great foundation came in large part from a man who once headed MAFAT, General Yitzhak Ben-Israel. He was born in Israel in 1949, toward the end of the War of Independence. Had Talpiot been an option for him when he was eighteen, he would've been a perfect candidate. General Ben-Israel has the intellect of a rocket scientist, the brawn of a special-forces commander and the confidence of a true military leader.

His studies focused on mathematics and physics (and philosophy, for fun). In essence, he was a Talpiot before Talpiot existed. His resume is that of a true unsung hero, a man who spent his life in the army without being noticed by the public at-large.

Ben-Israel joined the Israeli Air Force right after the Six-Day War in 1967. Before taking leadership of MAFAT, he held high-level positions in the intelligence and weapons development units of the IAF. He was in charge of the Israeli Air Force's Operations Research Branch. He has won Israel's prestigious "Security Award" twice for developing still-classified security systems. The first time Yitzhak Ben-Israel won the prize was in 1972 when he was just twenty-three, making him one of the youngest recipients ever. People familiar with the first awarding of the prize say it had to do with developing an improved weapons delivery system for Israel's fleet of fighter jets. The second time was in 2001. This award is even more clouded in secrecy than the first, but it reportedly had to do with his work on a major project involving the concept of fighting future wars. One official at Israel's Ministry of Defense (who could not be named for security reasons) said, "What General Ben-Israel developed is still one of the main secrets we have in our arsenal."

He also led the Analysis and Assessment Division of IAF Intelligence. In this position, it was his job to analyze how the enemy was thinking. In order to do that, he tried to think like them, putting himself in the shoes of Syrian, Egyptian, Jordanian, Iraqi, Lebanese (and later, Iranian) leadership.

He used these lessons often when heading MAFAT. During that period he was also in charge of the Talpiot program. General Ben-Israel would often refer to his work in intelligence in his bid to get Talpiot cadets to outthink their foreign enemies outside as well as their peers in other army units. Course work, lesson planning, special lectures and army service were redesigned with this goal in mind.

In order to accomplish as much as Yitzhak Ben-Israel has, you need to think a little differently from your peer group, and much differently from the average citizen of the world. And General Ben-Israel has worked tirelessly to help Talpiot cadets see into a corner of his mind so they can get exposure to the kind of thinking that has propelled the Israeli Defense Forces so far ahead of the nation's enemies in technology of warfare.

Every few years, General Ben-Israel takes time away from teaching at Tel Aviv University (where he heads the Tel Aviv University Workshop for Science and Technology Security) to lead current and former Talpiots on a week-long creativity sabbatical, where they can bond, share stories and information, and sharpen their creative skills.

During one of these sabbaticals, the group of young men and women from several Talpiot classes (some still active, some in reserves) were driven into the Negev and dropped off at an old air force camp. They were split into groups and told to come up with an idea of something they'd like to create, something that can be done in a week. The needed materials would be provided.

One team came up with a car deodorant that has the smell of a new car. The team was able to analyze the chemical compounds of that "new car smell" and reproduce it in a spray. Another team came up with a way to engineer a small box that could be dropped into the water tank of a toilet to cancel the sound of the flush. General Ben-Israel's hulking figure watched over the demonstration of this invention. He asked the young Talpiots why they'd spend their time working on something like that, and they replied that sometimes they phone their friends while in the bathroom – but it doesn't have to be obvious!

The general is gratified when the young men and women he's working with approach problems from an entirely new angle. He says, "We do a lot of activities like this to help encourage people in Talpiot to think in a creative, out-of-the-box way."

General Ben-Israel spent his career in the military thinking out of the box. After the Yom Kippur War he helped reanalyze crucial data. He still uses the lessons he learned to teach and demonstrate his different way of thinking.

For instance, before the Yom Kippur War, the intelligence community looked primarily for evidence to support their conjecture that the Syrian and Egyptian armies were merely carrying out exercise maneuvers – which was precisely what the Arab military wanted them to think. Ben-Israel recalls, "Yet, from time to time there were pieces of information that refuted this conjecture. For example, a few days before the war, the Soviet Union put the families of Soviet advisors in Egypt and Syria on a special chartered airplane and flew them back to Moscow. You don't do this if the army is merely carrying out an exercise. But the chief of Israeli intelligence said, 'Okay, I have so much information which supports and corroborates the exercise conjecture and I have only a few that negate it; therefore I think the most probable one is the exercise conjecture.' My method is not to look for supporting evidence. I look for refuting evidence. If he had adopted my model, he would have seen two possible conjectures here, exercise or war. We had strong refuting evidence against the exercise conjecture, the Russian families leaving the possible theater of war en masse. This should have rung serious alarm bells.

"In 1973, if the intelligence community, and especially the Mossad, had thought about refuting evidence more, they would have simply followed up to see that the Arab armies had indeed carried out the exercises they'd supposedly been assigned. They would have immediately found out that neither Egypt nor Syria ever actually completed the exercises. It was all part of a misinformation campaign. The Egyptians would send telegrams saying this unit should do that exercise, this unit should do that, knowing we'd intercept their communications. But we never checked to see that the armies were, in fact, ignoring the telegrams. That was a fatal mistake.

"In addition to giving credence to the conjecture that they were preparing for war, there easily could have been a third option: there might be fighting of some sort, but it might not be a full-scale war. No one thought of that either." Ben-Israel used his "refuting evidence model" and was proven correct. He concluded, "Same facts; different ways of looking at them."

Though former intelligence officers often get behind the times, General Ben-Israel's legendary, unique way of thinking brings Israel's intelligence agencies back to him, unofficially, even today. In late 2011, he had been analyzing "the Arab Spring."

"We collect a lot of data on what's happening around us. Sometimes we know facts, sometimes we think we know, then find different opinions. Sometimes we have what we believe are facts that later turn out to be not true. What is the relation between what you know, or think you know, and the decisions that you have to make?

"To make a decision, you have to estimate what will come out of that decision. For instance, take the Arab Spring. You read a lot about it. You see stories on television. You send your agents to these countries that are in the midst of revolution or to countries that could be the next to see revolution. You monitor it. You gather a lot of information. But what should we do about it?

"To answer that question you have to assess what will possibly happen with this Arab Spring. Will you get democracy? Perhaps you'll get a take-over by the Muslim Brotherhood. Will these countries go back to where they were after a year or two of revolution? You need to weigh all of the possible ways the situation could develop. Some people believe that if you study it long enough you may calculate what will happen, but I don't think so. There is no way on earth to judge what will happen in the future. It is a logical problem."

"Here is a simple example. You see one white swan, then a second, third, fourth, fifth and sixth. You still can't conclude that all swans are white. It's impossible, logically. Once you realize it is illogical, what will you do? Psychologically we were built to trust past experience in similar situations, but if we can't do that, how should we handle ourselves in the world?

"I think there is a way, though it is not in our nature. Nature built us to be inductive, to make generalizations from past experience. If you put your hand in a fire and feel the heat, you will never put your hand in a fire again. But perhaps the pain you felt in your hand might not be caused by the fire. If you were a scientist, you might check your facts by putting the hand in from a different angle, or putting the other hand in the fire. You'd do all sorts of tests. This standard way of scientific thinking can be limiting and destructive – even deadly – in the world of intelligence. For Talpiot recruits going into research and development or into intelligence units, as many have done, it's crucial to drop that way of thinking."

Thinking out of the box does not preclude learning from past mistakes, and this quality is a badge of honor to General Ben-Israel. During his time as head of MAFAT, and as the de facto head of Talpiot, he really pushed this point. To this day, when he lectures to a Talpiot class, he tells stories of past mistakes and tries to get the cadets to understand his way of thinking, so that they can learn to think differently from the way that most of us are preprogrammed by nature.

That's a key training tool not just for students going through a program, but for young men and women going through life.

Amir Schlachet, who moved on from Talpiot to major positions in the banking world uses Ben-Israel's kind of thinking to solve problems in his work. Though it may not be common for most people, Schlachat suspects that there's usually something inside a Talpiot that gives him the ability to think differently. "One of the strengths of Talpiot recruits is that they are multidisciplinary by nature – oh, and we're continuously curious." And as any teacher will tell you, the best student is often a curious student.

Chapter 8

Reality Check

*I*f academics are the backbone of Talpiot training, the central nervous system is the experience the cadets get going from unit to unit. In each unit-to-unit visit, the goal is to take the theoretical lessons students learned back in the classroom at Hebrew University and apply them to real field exercises and battle situations.

When the Talpiot program started, the military was adamant on one point: the students had to be a part of the IDF. Its early leaders knew that if the program were to be a success, the young cadets would have to see the problems faced by their brothers and sisters in the rest of the IDF so that they could come up with creative ways to help them and to advance the way the IDF works and fights, on all levels.

Students who had made it into the program soon began visiting the different units of the army, navy and air force to give them a feel for what happens in the field beyond the classroom. But because Talpiot was still a secret and because

77

of rivalries and suspicion throughout the various ranks, it was difficult to successfully integrate Talpiot students into the rest of the army.

Initially, the unit-to-unit visits were haphazard and disorganized. As there hadn't been much time from the moment Talpiot was approved to the actual start of the program, there was little chance to get the word out to field commanders whose help would be crucial. There would be a lot of "hurry up and wait" – boarding buses, then waiting outside checkpoints. Wherever the Talpiot students arrived, accommodations and meals were arranged at the last second. Even acquiring ammunition for various Talpiot training sessions was difficult. Though there were exceptions, the students were usually not made to feel particularly welcome.

The navy intelligence and technology units, however, were very different. Officers there were often more broadly educated. And though the navy was important, it was not seen as a unit with the history and glory of the tank units, paratroopers and the air force. Many of the early Talpiot recruits were given high level access to problems faced by Israeli naval officers and they were granted green lights to try to help. Several Talpiot recruits from the first three classes later performed extensive service in the navy.

Ophir Shoham was recruited to Talpiot's second class in 1980. He was a rough and tumble, serious student and soldier. A favorite among his Talpiot peers, they credit Shoham with bringing their group together.

He quickly became a legend during basic training with his fellow Talpiot classmates. A young recruit from a paratrooper unit was giving a Talpiot student a tough time. After a few minutes, the much shorter Shoham walked up to the eighteen-year-old bully and told the guy "go shove off – find someone else to pick on." The recruit refused and pushed him. But Shoham had already excelled in extensive premilitary martial arts training and the next thing everyone knew, the bully went flying through the air. He wound up with a broken leg and was subsequently dismissed from the paratroopers because he could not complete the training.

In fact, in those early days, many in Talpiot felt bullied and abused not just by other soldiers, but by field training commanders as well. Later, a special investigative panel sent by the Ministry of Defense would agree.

As Talpiot matured, a war was raging to Israel's north in Lebanon. Years of terrorist attacks on Israelis directed by the Palestine Liberation Organization and other terrorist groups angered the Israeli government, led at the time by Prime Minister Menachem Begin. (These groups had virtually taken over Beirut and other parts of Lebanon during a power grab in Lebanon's civil war, which began in 1975.)

Two attacks in particular were so outrageous the Israeli government felt there was no choice but to respond. First there was the hijacking of a bus by terrorists who had infiltrated northern Israel through the Lebanese border. That attack resulted in the murder of thirty-eight Israeli civilians, including thirteen children. Then there was the attempted assassination of Israel's ambassador in London, Shlomo Argov. The shooting left the ambassador in a coma for months. Though he survived, he was paralyzed and later lost his eyesight.

The war in Lebanon quickly became controversial in Israel, as many citizens felt Israel had entered into a full-scale war that had been avoidable. Many argued that there were other ways of defeating the wave of terror cascading from Lebanon.

For better or worse, war often leads to innovation, and in this case bright Talpiot students and Israel's military research and development arm were there to take advantage of the opportunity the war brought them. Lebanon became a military training ground for some early members of Talpiot. They were able to witness war from the frontlines – seeing which weapons worked, which caused problems, which systems needed remodeling. The Israeli military machine needed to come up with new ways of fighting, and Talpiot was there to help.

One system born in the war would later become known as "The Trophy." It is a tank-mounted anti-rocket device that is now in service on Israel's fleet of Merkava tanks. It automatically fires a projectile at an incoming anti-tank rocket to disable and misdirect the projectile, saving the lives of the tank crew inside. Talpiot students and a few of their instructors would become instrumental in making "The Trophy" operational.

As the controversial war settled into a controversial Israeli occupation of southern Lebanon, Talpiot's unit-to-unit program began to take form in more concrete and institutionalized ways. The army, air force and naval units started to come to the understanding that the Talpiot program was here to stay, that it was not a unit for spoiled nerds and that the students of Talpiot were indeed there to help them and future IDF fighters. They became more and more forthright in explaining their problems, their successes and their failures – and most of all, outlining how and where they needed help.

Cooperation and special training for Talpiot cadets became more encouraged and more accepted. Eventually, a very specific and organized program was devised to help give Talpiot cadets a real taste of what life was like in the skies over Israel in warplanes, in the hangars where the planes were fueled and repaired, in the trenches with the "green army," in tanks, armored personnel carriers, in the troop carriers that ferry paratroopers to their drop-zones, on ships at sea and even sometimes in actual warzones.

The training sessions with fighting units started to build connections between Talpiot and those units. Talpiot cadets would actually do the work of their fellow soldiers in the field. They didn't just learn about changing tire treads on tanks, they changed them. They didn't just learn about tank-mounted weaponry, they actually got into the tanks, drove them through obstacles, identified targets and fired. They flew in fighter jet simulators, they fired machine guns and artillery, they dropped off explosives with IDF engineer teams and they jumped out of airplanes with the paratroopers. They sailed on the sea with naval commanders and went underwater in Israel's submarines.

Soon the ordinary soldiers and officers in those units started to do review training with their Talpiot colleagues: they wanted more time to explain their challenges in the hope that Talpiot research would help them and their units down the line.

Ophir Kra-Oz spent some time in the United States while his father was an executive working in Georgia. He was inducted into Talpiot's thirteenth class in 1991, soon after Iraq attacked Israel with volleys of SCUD missiles.

He believes that going from unit to unit helps Talpiot cadets draw closer to the rest of the Israeli Defense Forces. "After you lift a 45 kg shell and you smash it on your hands and move it around, you can say 'okay, that's very heavy,'" he says. "Then you say 'let's try to make them lighter, but with the same power.' It's beneficial to see the problems on the ground. Though you're only eighteen, you see so many parts of the military you're really getting more information than most generals: they only get to see what's under their command. Most generals may be an expert on one thing and have their own department, but they never got this perspective of the army."

Spending time in so many units later allows a Talpiot graduate to think more seamlessly, Kra-Oz notes. "Almost all of the projects are integrated and that's a great advantage. Compare this to someone who studied something at university and went on to a company with a very specific focus. They get more and more specific as their career goes on. Although we [Talpiot cadets] come from math, physics and computer science backgrounds, we need to see how to implement the theoretical into real systems and real products which help the end user, in this case the soldier, but in an integrated way.

"For instance, take Iron Dome, an anti-missile system that targets short-range and medium-sized rockets. It was developed in part by Talpiot graduates from an idea of a Talpiot cadet. You need new technology and you need it really fast. It's a mix of at least five to ten different technologies. You have the missiles and the ballistics, but you need the software to know that this missile isn't going to hit a populated area. Seeing as much as we saw in the army really helped us understand how everything comes together and how everything is connected."

Saar Cohen, a graduate of Talpiot's fifteenth class in 1996, agrees that it was instructive to see the diverse needs of the military machine and the different technologies that keep it moving. "That was what I was most interested in from the start. I wanted to hear about military technology – and they were pretty open about it, with the hope that we would have ideas to make it better, more sophisticated, more protective and easier to use. By the time I was in Talpiot, they encouraged us to do a lot."

Cohen was also drawn to the camaraderie in the different units. "All units have their own sort of code, and this was fascinating to me. And more importantly, it makes you directly think about why you are working so hard. There are real people out there; and to some extent, just as we're depending on them to hit their targets, they're depending on us to break enemy code, to come up with better intelligence, to reconfigure weapons and to use physics to give them a greater edge in the field. It really hits you when you're out there. You're exposed to life and death situations and military secrets at a very young age. It's sobering to see things at that level as an eighteen- or nineteen-year-old. It quickly makes you realize just how important a part of the machine you really are."

Teamwork was another lesson Cohen learned from the army. About working on software programs while in the military he comments, "In most cases, you work in a team. There is nobody looking directly over your shoulder when writing code. But there are managers and supervisors, like anywhere else. Despite less supervision than in the corporate world, you have a serious amount of pressure in this kind of environment. But you always have someone to seek out and talk to for advice. Most importantly, people are always helpful on your team. It's a mission. Everything you do, every program you work on, is a mission and we all view it that way."

Today the length of the unit-to-unit training sessions varies from two days to two weeks, depending on the branch, the complexity of the unit's work, and how much help the unit might need in the future, according to research and development planners at the Ministry of Defense. Almost every section of the Israel Defense Forces will host Talpiot students in the weeks when they're not studying. There is no summer break for Talpiot. Most of the cadets will tell you that going from unit to unit is one of their favorite parts of the entire Talpiot experience.

CHAPTER 9

ATTACK BY KEYBOARD

*I*n July 2013, amid the Syrian civil war – while shells periodically showered on northern Israel, while Iran continued its production of nuclear material, while the political unrest in Egypt allowed Hamas to arm itself – Israel's top two military leaders found their way to a nondescript building hidden by trees in central Israel. The only armed soldiers in the area were the guards at the gates and doors of the complex.

For the first time in Israel's history, Chief of Staff General Benny Gantz (Israel's highest ranking officer) and Minister of Defense Moshe "Bogie" Ya'alon (a former chief of staff) attended a special ceremony for the men and women in a unit known inside Israel as "8200." In most armies, it isn't an everyday event for the top brass to visit a facility where minds are more important than brawn, where keystrokes are as important as firing weapons on the battlefield.

Unit 8200 is a fairly large, but elite, group of soldiers who work on computers all day. They can hack into just about any military network in the world. It is rumored that Unit 8200 can tap into electronic systems of enemies far and near, turn off power plants, radar stations and the electronic capabilities of enemies and allies alike. Unit 8200 has become just as important to Israel as the men in tanks and the pilots who fly F16s. One source familiar with Israeli military operations said, "8200 is now involved in just about everything we do."

The exact reasons for General Gantz and Ya'alon's congratulations to 8200 remain classified, but it's clear the unit had done something particularly significant. When General Gantz addressed the unit, he focused specifically on its covert role in intelligence: "Intelligence transmitted in real time enables the IDF to create a clear and accurate picture at all times and gives impetus…for sharp and fast action, which proves powerful on the battlefield." In his remarks, the Defense Minister added, "Your ability to identify threats in a timely manner leads to prevention. This unit is an example of the proper way to deal with frequent changes in the technological world around us. New threats create new arenas."

While scores of Israel's top high school computer students are recruited for 8200 each year, it is Talpiot graduates who play an outsized role in commanding and creating programs for this unit.

Among the responsibilities of Unit 8200 is the operation of a massive listening and signal intelligence-gathering facility capable of intercepting information all over the world. While 8200's capabilities are global, one of its main responsibilities includes listening in on what is happening not far from Israel's borders, in Gaza and inside the disputed territories in the West Bank. The unit has been credited with foiling scores of terrorist attacks and for helping Israeli security forces make preemptive arrests.

Reports still unconfirmed by Israel say that in September 2007 eight Israeli jets took off from a Negev air base. Their mission: destroy a Syrian nuclear reactor that was under construction in the eastern part of the country, not far from the Iraqi border. The jets were able to straddle the borders of several countries, including Turkey, in order to confuse radar systems. Reports from outside of Israel say that Unit 8200 also played a role by breaking into Syria's radar defenses and limiting its ability to see the incoming Israeli planes. The jets successfully fired their missiles and dropped their bombs before safely returning to base in Israel.

Soon after, reports from outside of Israel gave programmers at 8200 credit for scoring another major victory, this time against Iran's nuclear program. They had been asked by the prime minister's office, reportedly in cooperation with the Mossad, to develop some sort of a virus designed to infect, disrupt and spy on computer work stations in Iran that were being used to work on the Islamic Republic's nuclear program. Their answer: Stuxnet.

Stuxnet is a computer worm that was used to infect computers in Iran and was also used to give outsiders control of Iran's centrifuges (or at least to cause Iran to lose control of those centrifuges) as they purified nuclear material to a level used in bombs and or missiles. The United States also reportedly played a major role in Stuxnet; and it is congruent with US strategy to disrupt and delay Iran's nuclear ambitions without physically attacking nuclear plants.

Former Mossad chief Meir Dagan was asked about Stuxnet during a *60 Minutes* interview in 2012. It would have been treasonous for him to formally comment about Israel's role in such an action, but he smiled widely – prompting many to feel that was confirmation enough.

Since nobody has claimed credit, it's impossible to judge whether Stuxnet was truly a success. While it did at least slow down Iran's nuclear program, the program may have been designed to inflict more damage or to spy on the program over a longer term. So its overall success has to be questioned.

Stuxnet wasn't the only attack launched on computers inside of Iran's nuclear facilities. A virus called ACDC struck Iran's Natanz and Fordo nuclear facilities in the spring of 2012. One victim inside Iran with knowledge of the malware was quoted on an Internet message board saying, "There was also some music playing randomly on several of the workstations during the middle of the night with the volume maxed out. I believe it was playing 'Thunderstruck' by AC/DC." A UPI story on the incident said the message could not be verified, but it was believed to have come from workers at the Atomic Energy Organization of Iran.

Ophir Kra-Oz, whom we first met in chapter 5, had already moved on from the army well before Iran's computers were infected with this high-end spyware. But well before the Stuxnet computer attack program was launched, Kra-Oz, of Talpiot's thirteenth class, played a big role in Unit 8200. While in Talpiot, Kra-Oz was eager to learn everything about the IDF that he could. He took full advantage of Talpiot's unit-to-unit field trips, learning about the artillery, the armored corps, the navy, Israel's space agency, combat troops, fighter jets, radar and weapons-firing systems.

But his heart was always in technology. After graduating from Talpiot's academic program, Kra-Oz moved on to 8200, working on developing software that retrieved data stored in the Israeli military machines' computer servers. He described it as a "google-type search engine" for the army. It mined vast amounts of information for intelligence agencies and other branches of the military with specially crafted algorithms. The system could find very specific information very quickly and it was designed so that many people with many backgrounds could quickly understand how to use it.

Kra-Oz started as a programmer in 8200, then became a team leader and later one of the youngest section heads in the elite unit's celebrated history. Later in his career, in discussing his experience with venture capitalists, Kra-Oz pointed out that 8200 was a large unit, but it operated like a series of small start-ups, with different teams working quickly on different projects, although always in touch and in coordination with each other.

While the rigorous Talpiot program helped prepare him for 8200, the pressure was still intense. "In 8200 the military is physically very close to you, is very demanding and always has strong opinions about a project. We might be given days to do what we'd be given a year to do in civilian life. If we lost information, it could be critical; someone's life could be in danger. If you know that this guy is carrying a Qassam rocket and is on his way to fire, that's pretty serious. And I was able to help come up with programs that allowed the military to defend against those kinds of threats.

"My time in the army also taught me a valuable lesson I'd need later in civilian life: you have to delegate. There's no way to satisfy a military client because the problem is endless. You're constantly gathering information and insights from all over the world in many different languages, in real time, with limited resources. On the other hand, they had no financial string to pull as there is in the corporate world. Payments can be denied in civilian life. In the army the worst they could do was yell at me and tell me they were not happy."

A good number of other Talpiot graduates participated in vital intelligence activities as well. Born in Argentina, Adam Kariv often felt like an outsider after his family moved to Israel. Lacking many of the connections and networks other families had, he was convinced that he would never be able to be successful, as Israel seemed to be a place where connections are vital. When he saw a TV report about Talpiot, it clicked. This is where he wanted to go. Adam didn't think he'd get in, but he got through the difficult tests and became part of the eighteenth class of Talpiot in 1997.

After graduating, he was sent immediately to a technology unit of the Israel Intelligence Corps. He'd spend the next nine years working as a software engineer and then a unit leader. Everything he worked on remains highly classified, but it was his job to come up with new ways for the army to monitor events going on around Israel and to track people Israel needed to watch – from high-ranking officials to terrorists possibly planning attacks.

The pay he received came to about four hundred shekels a month; that's about 125 dollars. "Compare that to the thirty or forty thousand shekels a month you'd get in the private sector," Kariv laughs. "But you do the work to the best of your ability because if you don't get something done it could make a big difference in the life of someone, maybe a fellow soldier on the front line trying to protect you and your family. That's a very big responsibility and every day I did everything I could to do my best. Every keystroke meant something. It takes a while before it sinks in that your work could mean life or death. And even if it isn't life and death every minute, even in those times when it is less immediate and less critical, it is still very important."

Another Talpiot drafted into military intelligence was Haggai Scolnicov. "I went to a branch that is top heavy with great math and science people," he recalls. "It is a small place where mathematicians are needed. It was a shock to get there. There's a lot to learn and absorb. It's an amazing group of people. I worked on data analysis and algorithms. My unit had a very tight and specific domain which had been developed for several years. In certain parts of Israeli intelligence it is very well known, but it is not the kind of thing that gets much outside attention, and that's by design. Our base is north of Tel Aviv and it houses many similar units that have almost no connection to one another as we're not always supposed to know what the other units are doing."

Scolnicov is very proud of what he did in that unit but he can't share everything saying, "We're all quite good at talking about what we did without telling you anything we can't. We know how to work around the details." He continues, "No two projects were the same. It's very exciting. It's not like working for some client somewhere; you're doing something for your country. And you have an immediate, sometimes very clear impact on security and in the success of Israel's military. They threw a lot of important things at us. I was involved for ten years with problems that were generally considered unsolvable. We solved a good number of unsolvable things. Remember, in Talpiot they teach that nothing is impossible. They didn't quite mean it because, of course, some things are impossible. But they trained us to think that way. If you think differently about the question or find the loophole, you can move the unsolvable forward."

Uri Barkai also did his post-Talpiot service in an elite intelligence unit that served as a main nerve center for the

IDF. He came into the program as a software expert. Although his role was very important to Israel's intelligence-gathering machine, he was never given the full picture of what his work was used for. It remains classified.

Barak Peleg (of the twenty-first Talpiot class of 1999) went into signal processing. He was tasked with developing software to track radar, radio, computer and other communication footprints left behind by people of deep interest to the IDF. That includes armies throughout the Middle East and terrorist organizations including Hamas, Islamic Jihad and Hezbollah. All of them are becoming more sophisticated in how they use electronics and how they communicate with each other and with the governments that help them financially and with training. The list is long and includes Iran, Syria, Lebanon and many other Middle Eastern countries with close ties to terrorism.

He explains: "Signal processing would be obtaining the signal, digitizing it, manipulating it to handle whatever happened to it. If it's a transmission, how the medium affected it, and cope with what the medium did to it. This is for incoming and outgoing signals. The data would then be analyzed and then analyzed more in depth by army intelligence, AMAN. It could really give them a window into what was happening in places well beyond our borders."

Looking back on his Talpiot experience, Peleg conjectures, "The most important thing about Talpiot – which many graduates don't think about and the public doesn't know – is that they make us fearless. It becomes very hard to scare you. You can tackle anything."

In 2010 the task of tackling the unknown was given to General Yitzhak Ben-Israel, who formerly had been head of

MAFAT and a Talpiot lecturer. By then, it was crystal clear that battles were being fought between countries online and that online supremacy would be a key ingredient to any future military campaign. China and the US were already fighting battles online. China had been accused of breaking into the computer networks of American companies and stealing information, even snooping on highly classified military information.

Iran was also becoming more and more adept at cyber-warfare and espionage through computers. Computer hackers in the Islamic Republic broke into Saudi Aramco's computer system, wiping out key information. Computer users in Iran have also been accused of attacking the financial system in the United States and crashing or slowing the websites of American banks. Countries must be able to protect their financial and physical infrastructure from enemies using computers thousands of miles away.

General Ben-Israel was appointed cyber adviser to Prime Minister Benjamin Netanyahu. One of Ben-Israel's first moves was to create the Israel National Cyber Bureau on August 7, 2011, and appoint Talpiot graduate Eviatar Matania as its head. The goal of the INCB is to provide the prime minister with advice on managing this new and crucial front, where both defense and offense are needed and to carry out missions. It is also expected to provide for the continuation of "life as normal" if the country comes under some sort of cyber-attack, just like the Home Front Command is expected to do if and when Israel comes under physical assault.

Another reason for the creation of the INCB was to expand Israel's lead over its enemies in the Middle East in the field of cyber-warfare. As Israel's enemies grow their own cyber capabilities, the INCB was created to maintain that qualitative edge so critical to Israel's survival.

Matania was invited to a meeting of the Israeli cabinet in November 2011, shortly after he became head of the Israel Nation Cyber Bureau. He told members of the government that cyber attacks are "a broad threat to human society. While this is a challenge to the state, it is also an economic opportunity. The more we invest in academia and industry, the greater the return we will receive, from both economic and security perspectives." Prime Minister Netanyahu followed Matania, explaining to the Cabinet, "Israel is a significant force in cyberspace.... Just as we developed the unprecedented Iron Dome system that successfully intercepts missiles, we are developing a kind of 'digital Iron Dome' in order to defend the country against attacks on our computer systems. The INCB is designed – first and foremost – to organize defensive capabilities based on cooperation between three elements: security capability, the business community and the academic world."

In 2012 Matania built a national cyber situation room to assess threats launched against Israel from foreign computers. Its goal is to have one central place where Israel's political leaders can go to see the full picture of what is threatening the state and what's being done to protect it. It is also a place where high-ranking military officers, government officials and business leaders can come to share information.

The Israel National Cyber Bureau works closely with Israeli software companies to protect the nation from the growing threat of hackers working for hostile governments, terrorist groups, or working as lone wolves on the Internet.

Another of Matania's initial goals was to create clear and direct links between the bureau and computer scientists working in Israeli industry and at top Israeli universities including Hebrew University, Tel Aviv University and the Technion. This multi-system, multi-organization kind of project management is an approach Matania developed in Talpiot, where sharing information and cooperation are highly prized. He also instituted awarding funds to promising minds and programs in the cyber field. In 2013, $20 million was set aside for individuals, companies and universities with good ideas in the field of cyber-security.

Eviatar Matania has wisely used the bureau to help advertise Israel's prowess in global cyber-security, creating thousands of jobs and billions of shekels in revenue. It also serves as an arm that cooperates with friendly foreign countries and shares information about threats and enemies, much like Israel's intelligence agencies. The INCB also serves as a gateway for foreign investment in Israeli's technology sector.

In late 2012, the INCB took a new step: establishing a research and development arm. It was similar to the step the Ministry of Defense took decades before, investing heavily in research and development for Israeli made weapons. The research and development arm of the INCB is known by the acronym MASAD. It deals with cyber projects for both the military and private sectors. Israeli start-up companies, programmers in established software companies, university professors, members of the government and the defense establishment have all been asked to contribute to the effort.

As MASAD was announced, MAFAT director Ophir Shoham (another Talpiot graduate) issued a statement saying, "The plan is an additional layer in the Ministry of Defense's preparations to meet the cyber challenges currently facing the State of Israel. The MASAD plan is expected to link technological vectors based on the know-how and capabilities of companies and academia with common defense and civilian needs."

Today, through INCB and MASAD, Israel is always at the cutting edge of cyber development. Warfare has changed considerably since the 1948 War of Independence, when a clumsy, inaccurate canon known as the Davidka could turn the tide in battles simply by scaring the enemy with its piercing shriek and massive explosive boom. Its clever inventor discerned that when an army is outnumbered, ingenuity could compensate for lesser troops. In that respect, the creative and searching minds of Unit 8200 and the INCB continue to uphold Israel's resourceful military legacy.

CHAPTER *10*

MAKING AN IMPACT

*I*n the Israel Defense Forces, pilots and paratroopers get most of the credit for defending the nation. Tanks make up the backbone of the IDF. A highly visible Israeli navy patrols the coast on the Red Sea, and from Gaza up to the Lebanese border on the Mediterranean coastline. When it comes to intelligence, the Mossad is feared abroad and venerated at home. When violence breaks out, the cameras go where the action is. Reporters speak with the crews inside Iron Dome missile defense batteries. They film soldiers of the Givati and Golani brigades with machine guns slung over their soldiers, carrying heavy backpacks and ammunition. The media records the voices of helicopter and F16 pilots describing their missions while hiding their faces to protect their identities.

Talpiot's members are rarely interviewed on domestic or foreign news, and the program's massive contribution to all of those defenders of Israel is invisible to the public. Yet it's really the Talpiot graduates who spent so many years consistently helping to make the IDF and its impressive arsenal so effective during wartime and during the quiet times between conflicts. In fact, Talpiot graduates have come up with so many ideas, designs and updates to Israel's weapons and technology arsenal, an official count is not even kept by the Ministry of Defense.

The contribution of Talpiot to Israel's defense went far beyond anyone's imagination, primarily in three areas: research and development; the Israeli space program; and electronic warfare.

Israel's space program grew up alongside Talpiot. Its graduates have contributed directly to Israel's space program by creating space vehicles, electrical systems, communications systems and by working on the cameras carried by Israel's satellites.

In Israel's mind, staying ahead of the Arab armies and navies isn't enough. It also must stay ahead of the more advanced technologies from first world nations supplying weapons and weapons systems to the nations that pose a constant threat to Israel.

In the early stages, when the Talpiot project was first getting started, the navy benefitted most from its efforts, largely because it was more welcoming to Talpiot than other branches of the military. Just prior to the formation of Talpiot, the navy had done some impressive soul-searching.

It had suffered a terrible loss four months after the huge success of the Six-Day War: a brand new breed of Russian missile, fired by Egypt, slammed into the Israeli Naval Ship *Eilat* while it patrolled international waters in the Mediterranean Sea. While the crew of the *Eilat* waited for evacuation and rescue from other Israeli ships, Egypt again fired on the wounded vessel, sinking her. Forty-seven Israeli sailors were killed in the attack, another forty-one injured. Israel was shocked into becoming much more serious about defending its fleet at sea.

The six years between that deadly attack and the 1973 Yom Kippur War was very busy for Israel's navy. The sea force drilled. They updated their equipment. Officers studied the naval successes of allies abroad.

And it all paid off. The Israeli navy was one of the few branches of the IDF to perform exceptionally well during the Yom Kippur War. Though the general staff was starting to realize how valuable the navy could be, only a small part of the defense budget was earmarked for the navy.

When the first classes of Talpiot students graduated their Hebrew University course work many began to gravitate toward the navy. Eli Mintz had become an expert on data mining during his post-Talpiot military service. He was a pioneer in developing programs for the Israeli navy using algorithms to improve radar systems. Mintz says, "The Israeli navy was very small in the 1980s, but it was quite sophisticated. I was very motivated in the navy to learn and apply what I learned." To Mintz, it was a two-way street. He wanted to help the navy on its course to innovation, but he also wanted to learn what the people who were already there were working on and how they were developing state of the art hardware and software. "One of the best things about Talpiot," Mintz recalls, "was that after graduating, you had your choice of postings, assuming the place where you wanted to go would take you. Nobody else in the army gets to do that. So I picked a project in the navy where I did a lot of project management. It started with algorithms, but it evolved into managing certain aspects of a project from the technical side. I was able to wear two hats, doing real technical work and also project management."

The exact project Mintz worked on remains classified. "You don't develop i-Pods in the IDF. You develop weapons. We developed a weapon, which has since been improved by others in research in development." The weapon he worked on has been deployed, but it has not yet been used because Israel still hasn't fought the kind of extensive naval battle where such a weapon would be used. "If the weapon is used, it will have a big and immediate impact," he adds confidently.

Gilad Lederer is one of the most interesting and colorful of the Talpiot graduates. Lederer also joined the navy and became one of Talpiot's first combat officers serving on a missile ship. (His post-army work took him to Africa, including many countries in the midst of civil wars. More on his amazing post-army business journeys in a later chapter.)

Growing up in the 1970s, Gilad learned to sail as a boy and he always loved the sea – though that was not common for the average Israeli boy. After Talpiot graduation, his first assignment was to the naval academy. He served on a Sa'ar 4, a fast missile boat (about 400 tons and 190 feet long). He rose in the ranks to become a bridge commander before moving back into research and development. His operational knowledge learned at sea combined with his Talpiot training made him extremely valuable to Israel's navy.

Lederer went to work on developing and improving electronic warfare systems for the navy. Specifically he worked on "passive electronic warfare, defense systems designed to monitor the communications of other ships." Lederer also worked on missile evading electronics designed to help Israel's naval ships track and dodge incoming missiles fired from the sea, the shore or the air. "If you can mess with their homing systems, they can't hit you," he says cheerfully. He also went on to work in ship design, coming up with ways to make Israel's ships harder to detect with radar and harder to strike with missiles.

Ziv Belsky is currently a leader and innovator in Israel's still fast growing pharmaceuticals and medical devices industry. While doing his service, however, he was a true innovator. He also was one of the first Talpiot cadets to become a combat officer. From Talpiot, he also went on to the naval academy. His assignment was to serve as the executive officer of a Sa'ar 4.5 class missile boat, the most advanced in the Israeli navy. Belsky brags, "It even had two helicopter pads."

After serving at sea, he was transferred back to land at the Israeli navy's research and development headquarters. Somehow, during this time he managed to study electrical engineering and earned a master's degree. His job soon became to develop and innovate electronic warfare systems for use at sea. He and his colleagues came up with new technologies to defeat missiles fired at Israeli ships using electronic defenses. He says, "If you have a fast missile and you can shoot it down, great. Rocket to rocket. But if you have a system that misguides and tricks rockets, that's better and more consistently effective. You need tricks."

For Talpiot graduate Ra'anan Gefen, the navy also was the path to the Ministry of Defense's Research and Development branch. After Talpiot, he served as a naval officer, then began developing new radar technology and anti-missile systems. To move his ideas forward for the benefit of Israel and the United States naval forces, he shared Israeli naval technology with US-based military contractors. About his work Gefen says, "A ship must be able to defend itself against all threats. Radar is for navigation, to detect hazards in the water, to see other ships outside your line of sight. You need surface radar, to defend against airplanes and drones. Without radar, the ship is alone and in the dark."

But it's not enough to have a good system in place, Gefen insists. The crew must be able to use it properly. During the Second Lebanon War in the summer of 2006, Hezbollah launched a shore-to-sea missile (likely manufactured in China). It slammed into the INS *Hanit*, which was patrolling the Mediterranean in international waters adjacent to Beirut. Four Israeli sailors were killed, but the crew managed to get the ship back to Israel for repair work.

The problem in this case was simple. The officers on board the *Hanit* failed to activate the ship's radar and anti-missile capabilities, thinking Hezbollah lacked the technology to hit the ship – despite warnings from naval intelligence that Hezbollah did have a shore-to-sea missile capacity. To this day, Gefen is still dismayed over the decision not to use its anti-weapons system to guard against such attacks.

Talpiot has also had a tremendous impact on communications in the Israel Defense Forces. Because Israel is a small geographic area, armed forces transmissions can easily be picked off by even rudimentary eavesdropping equipment in Lebanon, Syria, Jordan, Egypt and Saudi Arabia. Developing ways to encrypt and keep those communications secret is a major priority.

One of the early pioneers in this field is a graduate of the second class of Talpiot, Boaz Rippin. His army service was dedicated to making radio signals impossible to intercept by the enemy in the mid-1980s. Israel was at war during this time in Lebanon – fighting Yasser Arafat's PLO, then the Shiite-backed groups, Amal and Hezbollah.

Rippin had never heard of Talpiot before being chosen for the program in 1980. He admits that when he joined the unit he wasn't sure it would work out. "It was a gamble. Nobody knew what graduates could do with what they'd learn. I felt like I was part of an experiment. The program was constantly changing."

Born in Tel Aviv, Rippin was eleven years old when the Yom Kippur War broke out. "An alarm sounded in Tel Aviv as rockets were shot at the city. Car lights would be dimmed. Apartment lights would be shut down so the city could not be seen by bombers above. I watched a lot of television. There were reports of people dying. I was worried about my father, he was a surgeon. He was waiting at a field hospital near Tel Aviv. I knew I was in danger. The fear of losing the war was palpable. People spoke about what would happen if we were conquered and defeated. No one thing shapes who you are but, the war did shape who I wanted to be in the army, to a large extent. I wanted to do as much as I could to help. This was part of the reason I decided to give extra service. I wanted to have an impact."

David Kutasov was nine when he moved from Lithuania to Israel, and he didn't speak a word of Hebrew. He recalls now, "It's amazing how quickly a nine year old can learn."

Kutasov remembers training with paratroopers in Arab parts of the West Bank and doing a drill where he and the other members of his platoon were supposed to sneak into the area at night. "The villagers woke up in the morning and came out of their houses. They spotted us immediately and started laughing at us. You have to understand that I grew up in Holon [just south of Tel Aviv], completely shielded from the territories and the Arabs. We were taught to ignore Arabs; not to discriminate, but just to pretend that they don't exist. Here I was in the West Bank, and all of a sudden it turned out that not only do Arabs exist, they don't like us very much. It was a big shock."

To this day, he's credited with changing the way Israel's ground forces operate. "The projects I worked on had to do with enhancing the fighting capabilities of tanks and infantry, using all sorts of advanced technology. I haven't been in the army in twenty years, but the problems I worked to solve surface today in Lebanon and Gaza. One of the men that was in the program with me and stayed in the army recently told me that something I worked on is now viewed as a bible for the people working in the tank corps – but I don't think I can say more."

As Kutasov discovered, for Talpiot grads there are no drills. Everything is real. You are given technical challenges to write programs or build something that is critical to the security of the state. That adds to the pressure and the desire to get the job done fast and done well.

Mor Amitai is a legend among legends in Talpiot. Many of his colleagues and Talpiot comrades say he can literally figure anything out. After finishing his Talpiot course work, designing communications systems became his focus.

A member of Amitai's team on a communication project for the army told of an instance when it was crucial for the IDF to know if the answer to a certain question was yes or no. The army would have to do things a very different way, depending on that answer. They needed to know if something specific was possible. "If the answer is yes, it is usually easier to prove. Something exists. If the answer is no, sometimes it is harder to prove. In this case, we were in between. We all worked so much and so hard on it that we all believed it was impossible. Sometimes when you try very hard at something and fail, it is very close to proving that it is impossible."

The project is still classified and shedding light on the specifics could lead to catastrophe for men in the field. The man on Amitai's team continues, "It was a program for a complicated system that should perform under different conditions. In the army, you don't control the environment. For one soldier in the field, anything can happen, even if he's trained well. He can trip, fall, or drop a weapon. This question was similar in some regards. It was a big question for the army. Will it perform well enough under certain extreme conditions? You cannot test these conditions unless you…" He laughed and said, "I really can't tell you more." All he could add was, "The army could not function well without it and it was something the army needed all the time. The army uses the system quite widely."

In his five years of service, Amitai was responsible for complex components of communications systems. Sometimes he worked on projects from scratch. Sometimes he had to alter something already in existence. And sometimes he had to combine different kinds of systems. A lot of the work was analyzing what can go wrong and how it can be updated in the future, as the specifications of different systems need to be updated for field use.

As in the example above, Amitai's work in army communications always had to take the unexpected into consideration. A colleague familiar with his work explains, "It's like a car. A car is something you can test. It goes well, air conditioning works fine, everything. But a car should also work well under circumstances that are not under your control. This is why manufacturers invest in crash test simulators to see what will happen when another driver makes a mistake. In the army, you also don't control the environment. The enemy is out there; it's worse than when you drive a car. Someone's not making a mistake – someone's trying to make you fail on purpose – to kill you and your friends. It's like building a car to withstand the tactics of other drivers who are trying to run you off the road. So when you design such a car, you don't have a full picture: you have to think what the other drivers will do or what the weather can do to you. We spent most of our time analyzing what we were building, to see if it will survive awful conditions."

Life and death are definitely motivational, and might intimidate some individuals. But Mor and his team were constantly told, "You belong to a small group of very talented problem solvers. The army has invested a lot in you. Talpiot is the longest course you can take in the army, even longer than pilot training and service. We've invested in you. Now go make us look good and don't fail."

Chapter 11

High-Tech Tinkerers

*I*ntelligence is where Talpiot has had one of its most dramatic impacts. Following the Agranat Commission's close scrutiny of the failures of intelligence in the Yom Kippur War, The Israel Intelligence Corps was created. The corps includes the famous Unit 8200 (discussed in chapter 9) which creates software programs, search systems and Internet defense systems to repel cyber-invaders.

The Intelligence Corps also works on tracking signal-based intelligence which includes monitoring radio frequencies, tracking telephone calls as well as other electronic signals. The corps also monitors and analyzes what is known as Open Source Intelligence. That includes monitoring the media in foreign countries including newspapers, television stations and radio broadcasts. In many authoritarian countries, the government uses state-controlled media to control its citizens, and sometimes sends messages to the West by way of their media.

One of the first intelligence field assignments given to a Talpiot graduate was in 1982. Opher Kinrot (recruited to Talpiot's second class in 1980) found his way into Israel's burgeoning new intelligence forces. "Israel was pulling out of the Sinai at the time. Prior to that, when they had bases and intelligence equipment in the Sinai, they could listen to and watch the Egyptian army. Now the army needed capabilities to access the same intelligence, but from farther away. I worked on making that a reality."

Another game-changing Talpiot graduate has become a modern-day Israeli Renaissance man. For security reasons his name can't be published. He's a tinkerer by nature, and since he was a child he has liked to build things. After graduating from Talpiot's coursework at Hebrew University, he declared his desire to be in "the real green army." Equipped with small arms, he would get his chance as a roving tank killer. He became Talpiot's first commander in the armored car division, and he set a sparkling example for others to follow.

For four years, his job was to track enemy tanks with small bands of soldiers and take them out, without armor and without a lot of back-up. As he moved up the chain, he was offered a chance to go to battalion commander courses. In 1997, he told the army no thanks. He would serve as a tank hunter in the reserves, but he wanted to get back to the technology that helps give Israel a leg up over its enemies.

His next stop was an intelligence technology unit. It all started with an interview with the head of the electro-optics division. "I remember he asked me, 'You finished Talpiot four years ago; now what do you want to do?' I said I didn't know. I knew I wanted to be back in research and development in technology. He took out a very small camera and said,

'Anything that you find interesting here?' 'Oh, I like cameras,' I answered. 'In my anti-tank unit I was actually working with cameras: signal processing, electro-optics and cameras.'"

It was a perfect match. He had the formal education and the army field experience to help design what was needed for other combat troops. This was actually exactly how Talpiot was supposed to work. A promising and motivated soldier gets an early and excellent education. He then hits the field. Afterwards, he combines both to help give Israel access to more efficient and more lethal weapons, making the army better and stronger.

"I started out designing a small board with a camera and signal and video processing unit, then on to larger components and larger cameras and optics systems," he continues. "The device I was working on was to be used for special tasks and missions. They were for the intelligence community, not necessarily the army," he says slyly. While he would not confirm it, it's likely the devices he worked on wound up helping Israel's various security agencies that monitor and police the hostile Arab populations living in cities and towns east of Israel's major population centers.

"We were making very, very tiny devices. They would put them where tiny devices were needed most. These kinds of devices helped many people to do their jobs. Many of these missions nobody will ever hear about."

One of Israel's most immediate and pressing problems comes from Gaza. While Gazans aren't a threat to the overall security of the nation, thousands of rockets have been fired from Gaza into Israeli civilian communities by Hamas, Islamic Jihad and other terrorist groups. Terrorists have attacked and attempted to break into Israel dozens of times, and on one occasion (in 2006) killed two members of a tank unit and took another soldier, Gilad Schalit, hostage.

In order to discourage border-crossing terrorism, the IDF set up a ring of surveillance stations to protect communities near Gaza, without having to engage anyone who appears to be approaching the border in a threatening manner. Brigadier General Eli Polak, head of the field intelligence corps, told *Aviation Week*, "Our job is to provide surveillance along Israel's borders. To do this, we use various intelligence, surveillance and reconnaissance systems which help us track the enemy and assist ground forces in quickly locating attempting hostile infiltrators." Here again, Talpiot graduates have played an outsized role in helping to develop and install sophisticated monitoring mechanisms.

Ofir Zohar (fourteenth Talpiot class) served in a technology unit in the IDF. He says, "The most advanced stuff in our circle was dedicated to building better technology for IDF intelligence. It was our job to come up with solutions for problems the army thought were impossible to solve."

Created by a team working on new components for tank units, the groundbreaking technology known as the Trophy System addresses one such "unsolvable" problem. Trophy is designed to protect tanks against rocket-propelled grenades and other deadly and more accurate anti-tank weapons. Israeli defense contractor Rafael, in connection with the Elta Group Division of Israel Aerospace Industries, has outfitted Israeli Merkava tanks and some armored personal carriers with it.

Trophy has its roots with Professor Azriel Lorber, who taught hundreds of Talpiot students the art of military technology during his nineteen years of affiliation with the program. Professor Lorber served in the IDF armored corps in the 1950s, rising to the rank of major. He received a master's degree in mechanical engineering from the University of Pittsburgh and then a doctorate in aerospace engineering from Virginia Tech. After his studies, Lorber moved back to Israel and eventually went on to work for two major Israeli defense contractors, Israel Aircraft Industries (which later changed its name to Israel Aerospace Industries) and weapons-maker Israel Military Industries.

Though originally rejected, the idea for the Trophy system was later adapted, modified and finally brought to fruition by Rafael. While the IDF was initially reluctant to install the Trophy system because of its cost, the Second Lebanon War in 2006 made it clear it had to move forward. Fifty-two Israeli Merkava tanks were hit by anti-tank missiles fired by Hezbollah. Israeli military leaders came to believe that the next war would be against a tougher, stronger, larger army that would put its tanks in even greater danger. If this is what Hezbollah could do, they didn't want to see what would happen if the IDF suddenly had to fight Hezbollah, the Lebanese Armed Forces, Syria, Hamas and perhaps even fighters from other fronts, all at the same time.

As Lorber had originally planned back in the 1980s, the tank has an on-board warning and radar system that is activated by incoming projectiles. Those projectiles are identified, and then a shotgun-like firing mechanism shoots a defensive projectile in buckshot form. The goal is for that defensive projectile to spread out its fire, connect with the incoming projectile and then force it to prematurely explode before hitting the outer shell of the tank.

In June 2012 the *Jerusalem Post* reported that State Comptroller Micha Lindenstrauss had heavily criticized the minister of defense and the IDF for not expanding the use of Trophy faster to protect more tanks, armored vehicles and especially the Namer armored personnel carrier.

During Operation Protective Edge in July and August 2014, Trophy got its first battle test. It successfully detonated and destroyed a Hamas anti-tank rocket, saving both the tank and the crew inside. The army has been tight-lipped about the details of that first successful combat use of Trophy, but in no uncertain terms a spokeswoman from the IDF says, "It has now been proven to be successful in combat."

The Israel Military Industries company, also known simply as IMI, has developed "Iron Fist" closely based on technology used in the Trophy. It is stronger than the Trophy in that it is capable of deflecting more powerful tank shells, not just the hand held anti-tank weapons the Trophy is capable of defeating. While the Israeli Ministry of Defense did approve usage of "Iron Fist" in 2009, that decision was later overturned; and as of now, the technology and the know-how behind it has been put on ice.

While the Iron Fist and Trophy systems are designed to protect Israeli soldiers in ground combat, usually not far from Israel's population centers, the long arm of Israel is the Israeli Air Force. It can strike without warning all over the Middle East and well into Africa. In recent years, western media reports say Israeli pilots have been called upon to hit targets carrying Iranian weapons moving throughout Africa, Syria and Lebanon, as well as weapons-making plants in places as far away as Khartoum, Sudan – eleven hundred miles away from air bases in southern Israel.

After his Talpiot academic career at Hebrew University came to a successful conclusion, Marius Nacht went on to work in aerospace. He helped design and manufacture airborne systems for the Lavi fighter jet.

At the time, the Israeli-made Lavi rivaled the F16 and the MIG. But there were problems. First off, it was very expensive. Should a country with only six million people spend hundreds of millions of dollars on making a fighter jet? Or would it be more cost effective to take the money Israel gets from the United States (after signing peace agreements with Egypt and Jordan, who also get US money for defense for signing those treaties) and buy proven, fight- and flight-tested American planes?

A second big issue was pressure from the American government against the project. The United States didn't want to compete with the Lavi in the lucrative international defense market if at all possible.

Israel always has been nervous about its reliance on other countries for defense. After the Six-Day War, France – Israel's main supplier for fighter aircraft – suddenly decided it was better to align itself with the Arabs than with Israel. France had been supplying Israel with Mirage jets made by Dassault. When Charles De Gaulle and France turned their backs on Israel, it was left with a true security crisis. Where would it find airplanes? Fortunately for Israel, the United States quickly stepped in to fill the void, as President Lyndon Johnson saw in Israel an ally that could be a check against Soviet aggression in the Middle East.

In part because of the trauma caused by the French, and because of Israel's expertise in aerospace, it decided to move forward with the Lavi project. Several Lavi aircraft were produced by Israel Aerospace Industries. The maiden test flight took off on December 31, 1986. Reports say the plane was remarkably responsive and maneuverable in the air, fast and smooth. But in the end, Israel's government believed that building its own fighter was neither economical nor politically expedient, so the project, while successful, was halted.

Nacht says, "When word came in the Lavi had been cancelled, I was upset. It was a phenomenal fighter and it could have been a game changer for Israel. Yet, at least many of the systems that are being used now are based on the system we developed on the Lavi back then. On a jetfighter, everything must be interconnected. There were many advanced concepts regarding interface. Now they're the standard, but back then they were on the edge. If we'd had to go to war, they would have made a huge difference."

A good portion of Nacht's work on the Lavi was on-board in-flight missile defense. "It was a very innovative and creative way of protecting airplanes from missiles. As far as I can tell, it's still not being deployed. The Department of Defense in the US now knows everything about it, but I think that system is still ahead of its time. There might be reasons why it is not being deployed now; there must be a good reason, but I don't know it."

Many of the things Nacht worked on, including airborne missile defense systems, were later adapted for use on Israel's fleet of F15s and F16s. Israel has a special contract with the American manufacturers of the fighter/bombers. In essence, Israel is allowed to install some specially designed Israeli components for communications, missile defense and radar. Intelligence estimates say that Israel has about seventy-five F15s made by Boeing and about 330 F16s manufactured by General Dynamics, all of which have Israeli designed and Israeli manufactured electronic warfare systems that advanced rapidly during and after the work done on the Lavi by engineers like Marius Nacht.

Similar arrangements have been agreed upon between Israel, the United States and Lockheed Martin, which builds the F35. All of the new F35 jets arriving in 2015 and later will have advanced Israeli electronic warfare systems. In addition, Lockheed Martin also agreed to buy about four billion dollars of equipment from Israeli defense contractors to install into the body of the advanced fighter/bomber.

Another Talpiot grad, Amir Peleg, worked on targeting mechanisms for Israeli F15s and F16s, though his primary work involved the research and development of high-tech cameras that could go on UAVs and tell the difference between different kinds of targets. "More specifically," says Peleg, "we built computer-driven vision devices that allowed for automatic target recognition. You want a gun to be able to distinguish between a tank and a car. We worked on things that are still in use in this field."

Zvika Diament is a rarity for Talpiot. He wears a *kippah* and is religiously observant. He is one of the few students to have come to the program from a yeshivah rather than from a secular high school.

During the interview portion of Zvika's tryout for Talpiot's sixth class in 1984, he was asked "How does an airplane work?" With a grin he says, "I knew that one." That question was prescient. After finishing his Talpiot coursework with the equivalent of three majors – physics, computer science and mathematics – Zvika went to work on installing and integrating Israeli-made electronic warfare components that were to be added to Israel's new and growing fleet of F15s and F16s.

He was the Israeli Air Force's representative inside a

defense company called Elisra (now a unit of Israeli defense contracting giant Elbit). During the five years he worked there fulfilling his commitment to the army, Zvika was involved in every aspect of development in new systems. He was just twenty-one years old when he started there, and Elisra was filled with more senior engineers who weren't always on the same page with what Zvika or the air force wanted. He notes, "It was very difficult, unpleasant at times. They were from a time before Talpiot, and they did things differently. They largely knew about Talpiot from news articles, but had no actual experience with Talpiot graduates in the workplace. Some were nice. Some were nasty and tried to get rid of me.

"I was stationed in the offices of the contractor. I had to define the acceptance tests for systems, and for each stage to make sure they were on track. I was in all the meetings, trying to provide them with solutions when we got into disagreements. And there were a lot of disagreements: They wanted to deliver what they had so they could get the money from the army, but sometimes what they wanted to deliver wasn't what we wanted. Over the years, they learned that I was sent by the air force and they had no choice but to accept me. The air force backed me up every step of the way, all the time, so they learned to deal with it."

Once the electronic warfare parts were made and ready to go, Zvika would lead the testing process. He often worked with air force pilots who had also studied to be engineers. This way they could act as both a pilot and engineer, determining what worked and didn't work, and why, during test flights.

Some pilots in the Israeli Air Force do their service, for about five years, then move on, but later serve in the reserves. Zvika's testers were some of Israel's most experienced pilots;

many had fifteen or more years of flying experience. That was especially useful because they were very helpful when it came to looking at the issue from macro and micro points of view. Zvika explains, "Let's say there was an experiment of a missile coming from one side, but we wanted the bigger picture. You take the aircraft and turn it 180 degrees, then 360 degrees, so you can see the level of the signal on all sides – where the signal comes in high, where it comes in low and where it is not identifiable. The pilot has to have a deeper knowledge in order to do the test perfectly. He needs to go beyond what he used to do to get rid of enemy aircraft or incoming surface-to-air missiles in combat. He needs a deeper understanding of what was working and what wasn't. That knowledge will save lives later on in a real fight.

"What we were doing is working with signal processing. You get the radar signal in your receiver, then you analyze the signal to identify what kind of missile is threatening you, a SA-6, a Patriot, whatever. For each kind of different missile, you react differently. For some, you transmit loud electronic noise to cause the missile to miss you. For others, you throw some flares to deceive heat-seeking missiles. You have to identify the missile threat within a few seconds to give you time to react to the threat. If it's transmitted from another aircraft, the pilot has to react within seconds; sometimes, after twenty seconds the fight is over. During tests we simulate the signal; we're not actually firing missiles. Sometimes you can simulate the battle situation with another airplane."

In the late eighties and early nineties, Zvika was working inside Elisra as orders were pouring in and Israel took more and more American-made F15s and F16s. Zvika was also tasked with traveling to the United States to make sure the specially designed electronic warfare system parts Elisra had manufactured were compatible with the F15s and F16s.

This was no mean feat. "General Dynamics (maker of the F16) would not give us warranties unless we tested our Elisra systems to make sure they were compatible," Zvika recalls. "The systems were two feet by two feet and you need several for each plane; they are in different places of the aircraft. They tested it as a black box to make sure there were not extra electronic current demands that could mess with the big picture, or that you're not sending harmful electromagnetics onto other systems, or that you're not delivering anything that could cause electric shock. They didn't mind if our system didn't alert on the incoming missiles. They only cared that our system didn't mess up the plane in a way that could impact the warranty."

Intelligence and aerospace are two core components of Israel's defense doctrine. If one falters, lives will be lost, as there is always an enemy waiting to pounce. Talpiot grads continue to play a major role on both fronts, due in large to part to their training. Their multidisciplinary approaches to complex problems and the ability to master projects that require teamwork and coordination are skills crucial to designing fighter jets and developing intelligence systems.

Former chief of staff Raful Eitan inspects the troops
(courtesy of the IDF Archives)

An early Talpiot computer science class
(courtesy of the IDF Archives)

Professor Novik teaches a Talpiot class advanced mathematics
(courtesy of the IDF Archives)

Felix Dothan, founder of Talpiot
(courtesy of the IDF Archives)

Gathering of an early Talpiot class (courtesy of the IDF Archives)

Beached ships in Angola during the civil war (courtesy of Gilad Lederer)

Gilad Lederer and crew on his missile boat (courtesy of the IDF Archives)

Gilad Lederer as a bridge commander (courtesy of Gilad Lederer)

The third class of Talpiot celebrates (courtesy of the IDF Archives)

Talpiot cadets train on a Merkava tank (courtesy of Avi Poleg)

Talpiot cadets receive explosives training in Lebanon during the First Lebanon War (courtesy of Avi Poleg)

Talpiots Gilad Lederer and Avi Fogelman rest in Lebanon during the First Lebanon War (courtesy of Avi Poleg)

David Kutasov, Talpiot graduate, in Lebanon after the opening stage of the First Lebanon War (courtesy of David Kutasov)

Talpiot cadet Avi Poleg (who would later command Talpiot), hand raised (courtesy of the IDF Archives)

An early Talpiot class practices a beach landing
(courtesy of the IDF Archives)

Amir Peleg at the World
Economic Forum in Davos,
Switzerland (courtesy of
Amir Peleg)

Talpiot's fifth class in 1985 (courtesy of Amir Peleg)

Elad Ferber outside the gates of Auschwitz on a Talpiot class trip (courtesy of Elad Ferber)

Gilad Almogy assembling a solar dish at his company, Cogenra (courtesy of Gilad Almogy)

Gilad Almogy discussing solar power with former United Kingdom prime minister Tony Blair (courtesy of Gilad Almogy)

Gilad Almogy with venture capitalist Vinod Khosla (courtesy of Gilad Almogy)

Detail and depth of a tunnel dug by Hamas stretching from the Gaza Strip into Israel (courtesy of the IDF Spokesperson's Office)

An Iron Dome battery in action during Operation Pillar of Defense in November 2012 (courtesy of the IDF Spokesperson's Office)

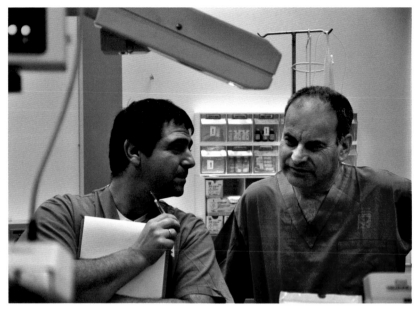

Ra'anan Gefen (right), working in the lab (courtesy of Ra'anan Gefen)

Ra'anan Gefen in the Negev desert for an artillery exercise with Talpiot classmates in 1981; left to right: Shlomo Dobnov, Opher Kinrot, Yuval Yehudar, Ra'anan Gefen (courtesy of Ra'anan Gefen)

Former chief of staff Benny Gantz and Defense Minister Moshe Ya'alon attend
a ceremony for soldiers of Unit 8200 in July 2013
(courtesy of the IDF Spokesperson's Office)

Adam Kariv (second from left) and cadets from Talpiot's eighteenth class pose
in the Negev during a training exercise (courtesy of Adam Kariv)

Ophir Kra-Oz working on a chemistry experiment as a Talpiot cadet in 1992 (courtesy of Ophir Kra-Oz)

Ophir Kra-Oz and team members from EMC in Israel outside their Beer Sheva office in 2011 (courtesy of Ophir Kra-Oz)

Members of Talpiot's ninth class on tank maneuvers in 1990;
left to right: Oded Govrin, Guy Bar-Nachum and Guy Levy-Yurista
(courtesy of Guy Bar-Nachum)

Talpiot cadet Matan Arazi in sniper training (courtesy of Matan Arazi)

Israel launches the Ofek 7 on June 11, 2007 (courtesy of the IDF Archives)

Chapter 12

Talpiots in Space

*A*fter Marina Gandlin graduated from the academic portion of Talpiot, she gravitated to research and development in Israel's aerospace industry. When missile attacks from Gaza once again began to escalate in December 2008, she was tasked to improve Israel's early warning alarm system so that people in Israeli communities close to the border with Gaza could have a decent chance of finding cover before impact. It was critical to design ways to make the alert system work faster: If there is only a thirty-second warning and it takes a full four or five seconds to detect a launch and determine the missile's direction, saving two or three seconds could save someone's life.

Marina explains, "My branch had responsibility for watching the skies of Israel – planes, air traffic control and everything else that goes through the sky. Since we have the radar for planes, we also have radar for missiles. I handled a lot of the launches and the hit points, which is very important because it lets you know which civilian population you need to alarm before the rocket hits. We were trying to help the army figure out where projectiles are going. I needed to determine where the missiles were going to hit and then quickly relay the coordinates. It was my responsibility to decide how many areas and how many sectors to alert after a launch."

After a series of launches, Marina would take the data from missile launches and where they landed, and enter it into a special computer program designed to help the army learn from past attacks. This could help determine likely strike areas in the future.

After a new cease-fire went into effect January 18, 2009, Marina began planning her next step, working in Israel's satellite industry. In 1988, Israel launched its first satellite, the Ofek (Hebrew for horizon). That successful launch turned Israel into the eighth nation to have a native satellite launch capability. Since then, nine Ofeks have been launched into outer space from Israel. It's believed the Ofek satellites make about six passes over earth each day. Israel also uses the Amos series of satellites, launched from the territory of other nations, often former republics of the Soviet Union. The Amos satellites are usually for communications purposes. The Ofek is not.

Its purpose is to take high resolution image photography of any place on Earth. The Israeli army and other intelligence agencies are usually the beneficiaries of what the Ofek satellites send back from outer space.

Gandlin's job in the Ofek program is to squeeze out every piece of data the satellites pick up. She develops algorithms to take advantage of the treasure trove of data and images that comes home. Marina laughs, "Don't think I'm looking at license plates or faces. In the satellite industry, people are laughing at this concept of being able to see faces and license plates. There's this movie with Will Smith, 'Enemy of the State.' You have real time images; they follow him with the satellites, you can see if he's sitting, standing or smiling. You really can't get that from satellites."

While Israel's satellite program does not live up to Hollywood fantasies, Marina says she's coming up with programs that help the army and intelligence agencies find whatever they're looking for, whenever they're looking for it.

While Gandlin's ambition was to be part of the aerospace industry, Kobi Kaminitz had no clue where his true interest was, until a routine class trip turned his life around. Quiet and thoughtful, Kobi's Talpiot commanders had high hopes for him the minute he was inducted into Talpiot's sixteenth class. They believed he could make a difference in Israel's future on a grand scale.

Kaminitz had other plans. He wanted to go into the army to become a fighter, a commander of troops in the field. He was all set to tell his Talpiot superiors – who had invested so much in his education – that he wanted to enroll in a field commander's course. It's not clear how they would have reacted and it doesn't matter. He never had that conversation.

One day, his Talpiot class was on a field trip to see parts of the Israeli space program in the works. When they went into a hangar and he saw the satellite Ofek-4, "that was really magic for me," he recalls. "I vividly remembered watching the launch of Ofek-3 on television. Then I was able to see another Israeli rocket launch in person. I knew then this is what I wanted to do. It was fascinating. You see it on the ground one minute, then a few minutes later it's four hundred kilometers in space. I knew I wanted to be part of that."

After his third year of Talpiot coursework, he spent the next six years working on the camera for Ofek-5. At the age of only twenty-one, he was working on a $100 million project crucial to his country's defense. When asked how he was able to get this top priority post, Kobi was extremely modest, saying, "Someone somewhere thought I was a good multitasker and was easy to work with." Of course, both of these qualities are extremely valuable, but Kobi had a lot more than that: extreme motivation to help his country, a desire to work hard and a world-class education in military technology.

On May 28, 2002, the Associated Press in Jerusalem reported: "The Ofek-5 reconnaissance satellite was successfully launched and will soon begin providing Israel with high-resolution images of the Middle East. Defense Minister Binyamin Ben-Eliezer said that the satellite and its launcher rocket, developed entirely in Israel, were 'a tremendous achievement for the Israeli defense establishment.' The Ofek-5 satellite, developed by Israel Aircraft Industries (IAI), rocketed into space onboard a Shavit launcher at 6:25 PM, from the Palmachim air force base. The Shavit's engines shot out a huge white vapor trail as the rocket sped westward over the Mediterranean. Minutes later the rocket and satellite disappeared over the horizon."

Looking back, Kobi says, "I remember the clock ticking down, from nine hours down to minutes, down to seconds. I was testing the camera to make sure that everything was okay in the monitor I was looking at. There are also a lot of different configurations you can work with. Exposure time, the shutter; it is just like your camera. The camera on the Ofek is a very complex equivalent. I could tell it to take pictures of this point on Earth, that point on Earth. You switch and test to make sure you can see the inputs – of which there are several dozen –

giving you different views. To play a part in this was really a great experience. When the first image from the satellite came in, there was nothing I could compare that to."

He then worked with demanding Israeli intelligence agencies after the launch to provide them with whatever they wanted. After a short time, Kaminitz was able to provide them with images without being asked, as he was able to figure out what they needed. Intelligence officers would often bring him pictures of other targets, asking him to check for updates on everything from weaponry to troop movement to the placement of tanks and missile launchers throughout the Middle East. The intelligence teams also had instructions when it came to optimizing the pictures of what they wanted to see, and they were very specific in requesting size and shading so they could be 100 percent sure of what was happening on the ground.

After working on the Ofek-5 camera, Kobi wound up leaving the army saying it would be difficult for him to find something as inspiring to work on. (Not long thereafter, he wound up using the skills he had acquired to work on very similar technology in the private sector to help patients in danger of losing their eyesight.)

Israel's space program and electro-optics are the expertise of Tal Dekel, of Talpiot's seventeenth class (1995). Dekel is currently a research fellow at Tel Aviv University's Yuval Ne'eman Workshop for Science, Technology and Security, which was founded by General Yitzhak Ben-Israel (the outstanding individual whom we met in chapter 7). The department focuses on a wide range of security issues through the prism of science. On the list is cyber-security, Israeli space policy, guided weapons, ballistic missile technology, nuclear energy and robotics to name a few. When it comes to space, the program focuses on using satellites for improving intelligence-gathering. While motives and intentions of a foreign leader can be debated, satellite imagery gives a clear picture of what's happening on the ground.

Through his work at Ne'eman, Dekel has been called upon to analyze the progress being made in space by nations in Israel's neighborhood including Egypt, a country many people – even those in security circles – didn't know had a space program.

Dekel isn't impressed.

Egypt says its satellite program is for scientific use, but many experts believe a country like Egypt – a nation with a questionable economy and a powerful military – wouldn't spend so much money purely for civilian purposes. Dekel believes that, as in most countries, their program is for dual use, military and civilian.

In 2007, Dekel helped monitor the launch of EgyptSat-1. Egypt was able to reach space with the generous support of scientists and space experts in the Ukraine. But by 2010, communications were lost with EgyptSat-1, and dozens of Egyptians who had worked on the program were fired. Dekel says the Egyptian government hid the bad news for months. Among his other responsibilities, Dekel often represents Israel at international and United Nations-sponsored space conferences. In the spring of 2011, he was in Geneva. He gave a presentation proposing international rules for the management and governance of space, rules that every nation would need to abide by to prevent one nation from interfering with another beyond Earth's atmosphere.

One example where space rules are needed relates to jamming signals. Many countries have the ability to stop signals from coming into their countries. (Dekel notes that Iran is actually a world leader in jamming technology and there's no way to prevent it. Dekel says you can retaliate by jamming their signals, but in the end, nobody in that scenario really wins: all that money that went into satellite launches and the sending back of signals is lost.) Beyond jamming, it is also possible to blind satellites with certain kinds of lasers – another area where international rules are badly needed.

A remarkable thing happened when Dekel presented his proposal in Geneva. Almost always, Iran's representatives – and the representatives of many Arab nations – boycott speeches given by Israeli experts at international conferences, including conferences run by the United Nations. But to Dekel's recollection, when he spoke, it was the first time that the representatives of Iran did not leave the room.

CHAPTER *13*

MISSILE COMMAND

We first met Ophir Shoham in chapter 8 when the Talpiot cadet launched a six-foot, two-hundred-pound paratrooper ten feet in the air for picking on one of his classmates. Since then, Shoham became the highest ranking and most prolific graduate of Talpiot in the military.

He rose through the ranks of the Israel Defense Forces, the navy (where he commanded a missile boat) and the Ministry of Defense to become a brigadier general in the reserves and the head of MAFAT, the Administration for the Development of Weapons and Technological Infrastructure. General Shoham also holds a seat on the all-powerful General Staff.

In this position, he became responsible for pushing forward missile defense. Israel now has defenses capable of shooting down three types of missiles:

- The Iron Dome hits short-range rockets. It was first deployed in 2011, but it became famous during Operation Pillar of Defense in 2012.

- David's Sling, which is not yet fully operational, but is ready to go. It is designed to take down missiles fired from 18 – 180 miles away. David's Sling is also sometimes known within Israel as Magic Wand.
- The Arrow System, the most complicated and perhaps the most important, was developed to defeat long-range ballistic missiles that could be fired from launch sites in Iran.

Shoham and Talpiot graduates have been essential in the technology behind each and every one of them. It was a perfect project for a Talpiot graduate, and many Talpiots inclined to this area of Israel's defense.

Missile defense is a complicated project that requires a major multi-discipline approach. Designers need to take into account the highest level mathematics, physics, radar detection, propulsion, explosive charges, the vehicle itself, along with communications – to name a few of the required disciplines necessary for successful missile defense. Then appropriate areas for deployment, where the anti-missile battery will have maximum impact, must be determined. And the people working on all those different areas must get along well enough to move the project forward together, quickly. According to a professor who was involved with Talpiot's student projects, the idea for Iron Dome was first dreamed up by a group of cadets in the 1990s, when Hamas began firing short-range homemade rockets and mortars at Israeli communities in the Gaza Strip. Projectile attacks on communities such as Gush Katif and Dugit became more and more frequent.

The rockets were very primitive, more like mortars, and while they weren't doing a lot of physical damage, the psychological effect on the population under attack was becoming significant. Retired Colonel Shaul Shay, former deputy head of the Israel National Security Council, says, "The government didn't consider these attacks a serious threat, but if you lived in Gaza and your home was coming under attack, you wanted it stopped." The question was how.

Hamas's rockets, later called Qassams (named for Izz ad-Din al-Qassam, who made a name for himself attacking Jewish people living in the Haifa area in the 1930s) became more sophisticated and more dangerous over time. From the mortar-like ordinance in the 1990s, they evolved into larger and more aerodynamic missiles, sometimes made with the long metal canisters found inside traffic lights, stuffed with explosives, nails and ball bearings. After the rockets were fired, the launchers could be easily and quickly hidden.

The IDF wasn't sure how to stop the attacks. They couldn't cover enough of the Gaza Strip from the air or by land to catch the men firing the rockets red-handed. After a missile firing, the terrorists most often blended back into the civilian population and hid their launchers, sometimes in homes, schools or mosques, and more recently in sophisticated underground bunkers.

It was a cat and mouse game between the IDF soldiers stationed in Gaza and small groups of nimble Hamas terrorists who knew the topography and cities better than Israeli troops knew them. Israel didn't want to send soldiers in to attack these small nests of terrorists every time there was a rocket launch. First off, it wasn't an efficient method. Secondly, most often they'd be playing on Hamas's terms and on their territory. Most importantly, the IDF would suffer casualties. In Israel, it's a front-page story when a soldier is wounded; it's the lead story on television news, and the lead story on news radio, which airs on almost every station in the nation at the top of each hour. Everyone in the country hears the details quickly and cares about him.

Hamas also had other ways of attacking Israelis. They left roadside bombs; they periodically inflicted shooting attacks, and starting in the early 1990s, they were able to terrify Israeli citizens with suicide bombings. These attacks really became a serious problem for Israel in 1994, when they almost exclusively targeted civilian buses, nightclubs, cafes, bars and restaurants, killing dozens of Israelis at a time and injuring even more. For the first time in quite a while, Israelis were running scared and were constantly looking over their shoulders.

After watching the escalating rocket attacks for a few months, a group of Talpiot cadets decided to focus their second-year class project on a fairly low-cost solution to stop Hamas rockets. It was a clever presentation, and it caught the attention of some of Israel's top military research and development officers. But the idea didn't go far in its first iteration. The military was not ready to implement such as system. But the Talpiot idea and the prototype they developed was a start.

In 2002, Ophir Shoham was appointed head of planning in the IDF. Along with the head of MAFAT research and development, General Daniel Gold (the man largely credited with developing the modern iteration of Iron Dome), Shoham pushed the missile defense system as a solution to the short-range missile threats. Engineers at the Ministry of Defense then began taking the concept of Iron Dome more seriously, believing it could be a realistic solution to a threat they correctly believed would only become worse in the years ahead.

Their plans ran into major obstacles from the army. Many

generals argued vociferously that it was the army's job to bring the war to the enemy, to be on the offense, not to spend money on unproven defensive measures. Fighting belongs on enemy territory, they persisted, not in Israel.

But in 2005 Prime Minister Ariel Sharon shocked much of Israel. The man known for "breaking the bones" of Arabs who threatened Israel uprooted the eight thousand Jews living in Gaza and forced them to move inside Israel's internationally recognized borders, or to Judea and Samaria, areas known in the West as the West Bank. Many in Israel and the world hoped this would be the first step toward peace with the Palestinians. Sharon himself called it a test to see if the Palestinians were really ready for peace; he wanted to see what would happen if they were given autonomy. The world quickly found out.

Hamas violently took over the Gaza Strip, destroyed infrastructure and greenhouses left behind and turned Gaza into a launching pad for Qassam rockets – and later for longer range, more sophisticated weaponry like Russian made and Iranian supplied Katuysha rockets that could reach further inside of Israel.

Between 2001 – when the Qassams were first fired – and 2012, there have been more than ten thousand rocket attacks against Israel fired from Gaza. More than 90 percent of those attacks came after Israel left Gaza.

Despite objections from many army generals, Defense Minister Amir Peretz (one of the least popular defense ministers in Israel's history) became an early backer of funding Iron Dome when he took office in 2006. For Peretz, it was an easy decision. He grew up in Sderot, which had been a constant target of Hamas rockets, and was extremely sympathetic to people forced to endure the dangers and disruptions to daily life caused by missile fire from Gaza. It was his final decision that allowed more funding to start flowing into the project.

In an in-depth article in *The Times of Israel*, Mitch Ginsburg reported, "In February 2007, with funding for just one year and without the requisite signature of the finance minister necessary for all multi-year projects, Peretz authorized the development of Iron Dome. At a midnight meeting in his office...he reached an agreement with Rafael defense systems officials: They'd 'scrape together' $50 million and the Defense Ministry would 'scrape together' another $50 million – out of an annual budget of some $15 billion – and production would start immediately." The engineers working on the project were able to show the Ministry of Defense a working model three years later.

In the meantime though, the rockets continued to fall. The attacks forced Israel to launch Operation Cast Lead at the end of 2008 through the beginning of 2009. Throughout the fighting, Hamas and other groups launched hundreds of rockets at civilian areas. The government was under pressure to find a solution to protect civilians from the constant threat.

Israelis in the communities within rocket range of Gaza complained that if the rockets were falling on Tel Aviv or Jerusalem, the government would have an answer: the army would retaliate harshly. There were calls for the government to reinforce the roofs of homes, schools and community centers to protect civilians. Many Israelis knew of the work being done on the Iron Dome due to news reports, and there was intense public pressure to set it up, fast.

In March 2011, the Iron Dome system was first deployed in the Negev desert to protect cities and towns closest to Gaza. The Ministry of Defense made the move with little fanfare, but a lot of internal debate. The system had not been fully tested:

it was called a "hot rollout" to further downplay expectations.

On the early rollout, Brigadier General Shoham was quoted in the Israeli daily *Haaretz* saying, "Senior defense officials were right when they made this decision; at the Administration for the Development of Weapons and Technological Infrastructure, we felt it would be proper to go ahead, even if the air force had reservations. It is not that they opposed this, but they were deliberating. We could have not deployed the system, absorbed casualties, and the politicians would have had less room to maneuver. In such a situation, we could have absolved ourselves by claiming the system simply was not ready. But the direction was clear and there was an excellent combination of operational planning and technological and logistical support. In my understanding, we were ready enough to take a calculated risk here, and it is not all that great a risk, because the trials were 100 percent successful."

Iron Dome is made of three main parts: a radar station, the control center and the interceptor battery which launches the anti-missile projectile. A number of Israeli defense contractors are credited with manufacturing the system, including the biggest names in the Israeli defense industry – Israel Aerospace Industry, Elta and Rafael, as well as many of their subsidiaries.

The radar, of course, tracks incoming missiles. But it goes a step further, telling the command crew which incoming missiles pose a threat to communities and which ones don't. Firing an anti-missile from Iron Dome is a relatively expensive endeavor. Hamas is able to make Qassams for a few hundred dollars a pop. The anti-missile projectiles cost Israel about $38,000 every time one is launched, so having the system prevent waste is important. But Israeli officials are very quick to point out that despite the discrepancy in cost between what

Hamas fires and what Israel pays to combat those missiles, if the incoming missiles hit cars, homes and neighborhoods, the cost of repairs would be much higher than $38,000, so you can't compare the cost, missile to missile. They also point out that $38,000 is obviously more than a fair trade when it comes to saving somebody's life.

Shoham also told *Haaretz*, "We have no pretension of intercepting thousands of missiles, only of gaining time, limiting the threat and in the meantime, the army is also doing other things. We must not forget that the system also contributes considerably to Israel's deterrent capability."

The first real test came on April 7, 2011, when a Russian-made Grad Rocket capable of traveling twenty-five miles was fired from Gaza in the direction of Beer Sheva, the largest city in southern Israel, home to 200,000 people.

Those who witnessed history being made say the Iron Dome's radar picked up the incoming missile. The system tracked it, and within milliseconds determined it would likely hit a populated area. Sirens wailed, lights flashed, the young men and women in the command center began shouting commands and following orders. The anti-missile was launched. With a short, loud explosion, it shot into the air. Three seconds, four seconds, five seconds...ten seconds later an explosion could be seen in the sky, followed by a loud boom. Success. At a cabinet meeting a few days later, Prime Minister Netanyahu said, "Israel marked a significant and impressive achievement with the Iron Dome system intercepting missiles. This has echoed throughout the world." More successful interceptions would follow in the weeks and months ahead.

The army reports that during the April 2011 escalation with Gaza, the Iron Dome had a 65 percent success rate. That was the month the system began operating. In August 2011, during another round of missile attacks, the Iron Dome's success rate hit 70 percent. In March 2012, Iron Dome had an 80 percent success rate. In June 2012, the Iron Dome's hit rate reached 85 percent. In October of that year, the success rate hit 95 percent.

More rocket attacks, and Hamas's acquisition of missiles that could hit Tel Aviv, led to a new round of intense fighting in November 2012, with Israel launching Operation Pillar of Defense. During Operation Pillar of Defense, 1,506 rockets were fired at Israel from Gaza. The Iron Dome system determined that 421 of those rockets were a threat, and 85 percent of those threats were destroyed in mid-air. The Ministry of Defense says it does not keep exact statistics on successful launches, but they do believe that with some tweaking, the system can be close to 100 percent effective in the years to come. There is optimism within Israel's defense community that the Iron Dome will be sought after by other countries and will add to the Israeli-made weapons systems the country sells and exports. As of winter 2015, no agreements have been signed.

While Talpiot originally dreamed up the system and the highest ranking Talpiot grad, Ophir Shoham, was partially responsible for making it happen (with the help of the Israeli military industry), the United States was a big factor in paying for Iron Dome. Congress approved about $500 million in funding for the project; and in June 2013, lawmakers tacked on another $15 million in funding, in the hope that the US could collaborate directly in future developments. That same month, the House of Representatives' Armed Services Committee approved $284 million to help pay for programs designed to team up with Israel in the field of missile defense.

Israel and the United States have been working together

on longer range missile defense systems for decades. The two jointly developed the Arrow anti-missile system.

The Arrow is now in its third generation and is mainly designed with the threat of Iran's ballistic missile program in mind. It is considered to be the world's best long-range missile interceptor.

Production of the Arrow began in 1986, the same year Talpiot students were starting to make a name for themselves in Israel's space program. Israel's space scientists made a huge contribution to the Arrow because, in effect, it is a rocket. The Arrow is tasked with streaking approximately thirty miles above the earth's surface, seeking out incoming missiles and then exploding, knocking out the enemy projectile. One of its many goals is to destroy an incoming missile armed with nuclear, biological, or chemical warheads far enough into the sky that the deadly payload doesn't hit Israel.

The Arrow is jointly developed by Boeing and Israel Aerospace Industries at a cost of about $3 million per missile. The rockets run on solid fuel rather than more volatile liquid fuel. Solid fuel also gives the Arrow missile commanders the luxury of not having to deploy the rockets shortly before they're used; in other words, they're always ready to go on the launch-pad. That's key because missile defense often can't be planned. An interceptor like the Arrow is only used when an enemy fires its missiles, so timing is unpredictable, to put it mildly.

Like the Iron Dome system, the rocket launchers don't operate independently. Instead, there is a command center, a separate radar station and the battery that actually fires the missiles.

The Arrow 1, 2 and 3 have all been successfully test-fired

in actual simulations, and the system has proven it can take out enemy missiles. In test phases, physicists, engineers and Israeli soldiers manning the Arrow batteries claim the Arrow has a 90 percent success rate.

Many in the world of aerospace, including some Israeli experts, have long doubted the effectiveness of the Arrow. Some in the Israeli defense establishment have even said the billions of dollars spent on the Arrow system would be better used elsewhere. Others say the Arrow might work, but could be defeated with decoys. That is to say if an enemy country fired fifty missiles at Israel and only one was armed with a nuclear warhead, with the other forty-nine being decoys, the Arrow would not be able to save the day.

One Israeli physicist with in-depth knowledge of the capabilities of the Arrow, who also teaches in the Talpiot program, laughs off those fears. He agrees missile defense will never be 100 percent effective, but decoys can most definitely be defeated.

Professor Azriel Lorber, a Talpiot teacher for almost two decades, attests, "Former students of mine from Talpiot worked on solving the decoy dilemma in the Arrow's early years. Decoys show off different flight characteristics, giving them away. It is also true that it's easier and cheaper for the enemy to build a real missile than to build a good decoy. All of these factors are helpful in determining which is the real thing and which isn't."

The first Arrow battery was installed at Palmachim Air Base south of Tel Aviv. Several successful test launches and test interceptions have been executed from this base. While the Arrow has not been used in a real life situation, the officers who would be the ones firing at an enemy missile have been able to test a lot of their skills during the civil war in Syria.

The Syrian army launched several Scud missiles in their attempt to quash the rebel uprising that began in 2011. Israel initially became very familiar with Scuds during the First Gulf War, when Saddam Hussein fired three dozen of them at Israel in 1991.

In 2011, 2012 and 2013, Syria's firing of Scuds set off alarm bells at Palmachim Air Base, forcing anti-missile teams to have their fingers on the triggers, as radar tracked those launches inside of Syria.

When Syria fires its Scuds, Israel tracks those missiles. They're doing it in part to test their tracking abilities and to study the way Syria fires the Scuds, but most importantly, Israel tracks them to make sure they're not being fired at Israel. The Ministry of Defense says that for the first few critical seconds it is difficult to tell if attacks that go from north to south are aimed at rebel held areas in Syria or if Israel is the target.

In 2013, Colonel Zvika Haimovich told Reuters news service that after Bashar al-Assad's forces fire a missile, Israel only has a few seconds to determine it if is the target or not. "Syria's batteries are in a high state of operability, ready to fire at short notice. All it would take is a few degrees' change in the flight path to endanger us." In that same article, Colonel Haimovich also told Reuters, "We are looking at all aspects, from the performance of the weaponry to the way the Syrians are using it. They have used everything that I am aware exists in their missile and rocket arsenal. They are improving all the time, and so are we, but we need to study this and to be prepared."

The Reuters report continues: "Long-range radars feed real-time data on the barrages to Haimovich's command bunker, where officers brace to activate Arrow II, a US-backed Israeli missile shield that has yet to be tested in battle. The more threatening launches set off sirens across Palmachim, whose warplanes also await orders to scramble. Haimovich would not detail how Israel determines a missile fired in its direction will not cross the border, saying only that the process took 'more than a few seconds, but not much more.' Another Israeli expert, speaking on condition of anonymity, said it combined split-second analysis of the strength of the launch with up-to-date intelligence on Assad's intentions."

Israel also has developed a missile interceptor that's able to detect, track and destroy medium range rockets heading into Israel. David's Sling had its first successful test on November 25, 2012. It is in its final test stages and hopefully will be deployed in time for Israel's next inevitable war.

It will be expected to take out rockets fired from up to 150 miles away. That would put missiles fired by terrorists, or anyone else, from Egypt's Sinai desert within range. Over the past several years, dozens of missiles have targeted the Israeli port city of Eilat.

The system, however, was designed with Syria and Lebanon in mind. Syria has missiles capable of striking anywhere in Israel. Lebanon is host to Hezbollah, which boasts it can hit anywhere in Israel with its impressive missile arsenal. In order to bring about a cease-fire after the Second Lebanon War in the summer of 2006, the international community pledged to prevent Hezbollah from rearming. Despite that, Hezbollah is believed to have more than forty thousand missiles aimed at Israel and ready to go.

Hezbollah possesses three main missiles, the Zelzal and the Fatteh 110. Both are made and supplied by Iran. *Zelzal* is Persian for earthquake, *fatteh* means conqueror. The third missile category is the Russian made Katyusha.

The Zelzal and Fatteh-100 are both capable of carrying fifteen-hundred-pound warheads and have an approximate range of 150 miles. That would put both missiles in the "killable" category for David's Sling. Syria also possesses the Fatteh-110, and reports say the Syrian army controlled by Bashar al-Assad has used them against rebels during Syria's civil war.

The Katyusha is not as advanced as the Fatteh-110 or the Zelzal, but it packs a major punch. It was used heavily by Hezbollah during the Second Lebanon War. It poses a threat to Israel because the missiles are often fired from mobile launchers. They can be fired quickly and in heavy volumes, then hidden from Israeli aircraft.

David's Sling's is capable of dealing with all three of those missiles, and its main responsibility will be to prevent Hezbollah's missiles from damaging Israeli communities. With targeting and guidance devices implanted in the nose, David's Sling interceptor missile is sometimes known as "The Stunner." Compared to the Arrow missiles, the interceptor fired by David's Sling is less expensive.

There is no doubt that Israel's sophisticated missile defenses will be of critical importance in the years ahead, as constant research and upgrading in this field will provide a much needed sense of security for all of its citizens. Its cutting-edge development and far reaching impact in large part reflect the work of Talpiot cadets and Talpiot graduates, not the least of whom is the visionary Brigadier General Ophir Shoham.

CHAPTER 14

ON A MISSION

G iora Kornblau always wanted to fly. When it came time
to serve in the IDF, he was certain he'd shoot for flight
school. Giora wanted the air force. But Talpiot wanted Giora.

As his three years of study started coming to a close, he
opted to postpone working in research and development, the
destination for most Talpiot graduates, and join the air force.
He wanted to be a fighter pilot. Colonel Avi Poleg, who headed
Talpiot at the time, usually encouraged graduates to consider
combat service after graduation. When he and his staff would
find a candidate for that kind of route, he would help the Talpiot
graduate navigate the bureaucratic maze leading to combat
posts. "I find the combination of Talpiot and combat service to
be an excellent way to get involved in major important domains
in the defense area," says Poleg. "After serving a period in the
field, there is a potential for building a long and stable military
career, which may lead to the top."

This was certainly the case for Kornblau, one of the first
Talpiot graduates to go on to flight school. Born in Argentina
in 1972, he was brought to Israel by his family one year later.

When Talpiot recruited him, he had not heard of the program, but he would soon join as part of the twelfth class, inducted in 1990.

When Kornblau announced his intention to go to flight school, there was no precedent for making such a move. All the rules were being written as Giora moved forward. Part of his argument was that for three years Talpiot had pressed upon his class the importance of combat training and the importance of "getting your hands dirty in the field. They want people with a combination of an education and real combat experience. I agreed with them."

He remembers, "There were some bureaucratic hurdles. There are always roadblocks, but everyone always comes together at the last minute. I did need to do some convincing at the Ministry of Defense, which had invested in my education. At the end of Talpiot, there is a three month graduation project. In order to start flight school after graduating I needed to miss that. There was a lot of discussion, but in the end the Ministry of Defense and the leaders of Talpiot said, 'If you pass flight school, go ahead into the air force.' The air force, however, was very black and white about the whole issue. They said, 'We don't need convincing, we just need you to pass the test.'"

And like almost everything else Kornblau had done to this point in his life, he was a success. After passing his initial tests, the learning curve steepened. He began learning to fly combat style missions on A4 Skyhawks, now used for training in the Israeli Air Force. The planes were previously used by Israel in combat missions in the late 1960s and early 1970s, as well as in the early 1980s in Operation Peace for the Galilee. As "flying artillery," their main mission was to pound ground targets and provide cover for Israel's ground forces.

After mastering the A4s, he was taught to fly F16s. The F16 is known as Israel's long arm. Israel's fleet of about 225 F16s can be refueled in mid-air and have been known to be capable of striking anywhere in the Middle East to the northern half of Africa, which has become a travel route for weapons sold to Hamas and other terrorist networks in Gaza and the Sinai.

In June 2008, one hundred Israeli F16s and F15s flew in formation toward Greece. The distance is about nine hundred miles, the same distance from Israel to Iran. Greece is armed with the Russian-made SA-300 anti-aircraft system, the same system Russia was reportedly considering selling to Iran. The point the Israeli Air Force was making was pretty blunt: it is ready to carry out any mission anywhere, at any time.

The missions of Israeli Air Force pilots usually remain classified for decades after they've been carried out. Kornblau could only say he was called on to carry out missions in all the areas where the Israeli Air Force was active during his time as a pilot. During his time in service, the IAF carried out bombing missions against Hamas and Islamic Jihad in Gaza, after both organizations had launched wave after wave of terrorist attacks against Israeli civilians. Israel also began targeting the leaders of those terrorist operations in an effort "to cut off the head of the snake."

Another theater of operation during Kornblau's time in the air force was to the north of Israel, in Lebanon. He flew during the final months of the Israeli army's occupation of southern Lebanon (which had begun in 1982). As the Lebanon-based PLO became less of a nuisance for Israel, Iranian-backed Hezbollah took over as "resistance fighters," providing the IAF with targets for years to come.

Since the early days, the fighter pilot has been known as

"a thinking man's warrior." You need to know how to operate the complicated controls, how to not stall in midair; you need to know physics and aerodynamics. You need to surmise what your opponent is able to do and when he will do it. Once in the air, Israeli Air Force pilots are given a lot of leeway to accomplish their mission. Despite his combat experience, Kornblau admits to being embarrassed when asked what he thinks about while flying missions. "I don't regard myself as a brave pilot with brave stories to tell. Usually I'm thinking of many things. Some are related to the mission and how to perform it the best I can, simulating in my mind the critical parts of the mission and what needs to be done. And sometimes I think about lunch, or anything else that pops into my mind. I think it's the same for anyone else about to perform something that's important to them."

After finishing his time as a fighter pilot in the most advanced plane in the Israeli Air Force's arsenal, Kornblau took the knowledge he acquired and moved back to research and development. He said, "The experience gave me the technical knowledge to be able to work on the future of the air force – and to help develop the technologies of the future."

Arik Czerniak is one of Talpiot's most popular graduates. As a competitive teenager, he and his friends were in a constant state of one-upmanship to see who could get into the best army unit. Czerniak wanted to win, but he discounted Talpiot, thinking he'd never get in. So he set his sights on becoming a fighter pilot.

As draft day approached, he was invited to come to Talpiot's early testing. When he got there, the officers asked him what he wanted to do. Czerniak was forthright: "'I want to be a fighter pilot."

"No problem," they laughed, "you can do both."

"They sent me to the committee, a testing panel," recalled Czerniak. "One week before, I had read a book about Einstein's theory of relativity in order to try to look prepared and smart. Everyone needed to prepare something scientific to talk about. Then we talked about physics. They asked me how a solar-powered boiler works, the ones on the roof. They asked me what I would want to study if I weren't in the army, and I said architecture. Then they asked me an architectural problem and I had to show them how I'd plan a living room. Then they asked me a progression problem. I even remember it: 61 55 52 63 94…what's the next number?

"I stood up at the white board and tried all the various mathematical methods I knew to solve progressions, and they said, 'Just flip the order of the digits,' and I said, '…oh, right.' I looked like an idiot, but it was funny. It was just a trick. Looking back, they just wanted to see how well I could handle pressure.

"At the end of the testing I asked again, 'Can I still be a pilot?' I wanted to ask as many people as possible, to make sure the answer would always be yes, and it was. They were true to their word."

While he was waiting to hear back from Talpiot, he accepted an invitation to try out for pilot school. "In the air force, the training was seven days, with six hundred people. They put you in uniform. You spend the day running around, completing orders. There's no English word for what we had to do, but it translates to 'advancement by the legs.' You see that tree? You have twenty seconds to run there and back: GO! You didn't make it. Do it again! There were a lot of group activities and tests like digging holes, solving puzzles, hanging from monkey bars; everyone hangs and you see who falls first and last. There's really no sleeping, they woke us up after a two-hour rest."

Czerniak made it past all the hurdles. But in the end he thought to himself, "Thanks, guys, this is a good failsafe, but now I'm really hoping to get into Talpiot." As he graduated high school, he still didn't have an answer from Talpiot. One day in the early summer, he was playing on his computer when the call came in. "Congratulations, you've been accepted to Talpiot's fifteenth class." His first question – "Can I still be a pilot?"

His first day in Talpiot, the commanders brought the cadets pitas and schnitzel. "Then wham! It was off to paratrooper training. After six days, I could barely move my legs, but I kept going and going. It was a piece of cake compared to what my friends in combat units did, but it was still hard."

When classes began, the course load was really heavy. But Czerniak had an ace up his sleeve. He'd always had the ability to concentrate on material in the hours right before a test and to do well. After graduating from Hebrew University and Talpiot's academic program, Czerniak was expected to do six months of research and development before doing anything else. It had already been mapped out. His job would be to work on a new Israeli-made radar system for F16s, systems the Israeli air force would install into the American-made fighter jets.

But the air base commander where he would serve said, "Enough is enough. If you want to be a pilot, you have to come *now*." The bureaucratic barriers were crossed, the documents were signed and Arik Czerniak was off to start army service again from the very bottom. (The Ministry of Defense later marked this as a bad decision. In the years afterward, with few exceptions, Talpiot graduates would have to do some work in research and development before moving on to fighting units.)

Czerniak was finally learning to fly. After graduating flight school, he was given the keys to an F4 Phantom Jet, a fighter bomber once used heavily by the IAF. But soon after he had been assigned to an F4 squadron, the air force decided the plane had seen its best years. Czerniak was disappointed, but happy with his new assignment. To this day, he's a flight instructor in an A4 Skyhawk. Like the F4, the A4 was once a big part of the Israeli Air Force's fighting fleet. The flying skills Czerniak learned in those now outdated planes have still been put to great use. "I go to reserves a day or two every two or three weeks to train pilots in air-to-air combat. I usually teach dogfights. If tomorrow two F16s – one from Egypt, one from Israel – would get in close range there would be a dogfight. The dogfighting I teach is like teaching someone to dribble. You're not firing bullets, of course. Your goal is to take a picture of the other guy in your gun sights. You're behind him, three hundred meters, he's squiggling in your gun sight, and it's all captured on video. When you go down, you debrief to find out who won, who lost, and why."

Many of the graduates of Talpiot humbly say no matter what their contribution is to the security of Israel, nothing ever outweighs the sacrifice made by a real fighter, a soldier on the frontlines, a fighter pilot flying over enemy territory, or a sailor engaging in battle on the sea.

Boaz Rippin of Talpiot's second class knew one incredibly smart young recruit in Talpiot who came from a kibbutz. Rippin said, "After a few weeks, he quit. He felt that he couldn't go back to his kibbutz in the uniform of a jobnick." A "jobnick" refers to a soldier in the Israeli military who doesn't directly fight. He might have a desk job in logistics, or in intelligence, or work in the IDF's public relations unit – all are important jobs that make the army and the country run – but they're not seen as risking their lives for their country. "The army will always put those who risk their lives on a higher platform. The most extreme case is the fighter pilot. They are looked at differently, and always will be," according to Rippin.

Of the approximately seven hundred Talpiot graduates, several decided to move into combat positions, deferring work in research and development or other more traditional Talpiot post-graduation jobs.

One of those soldiers came through Talpiot's eleventh class. Because of his role in the Talpiot program and IDF service, Israel's Ministry of Defense would not allow his name to be published. He would later become a commander of Talpiot, but before that he worked his way into one of the IDF's most daring units, Shaldag. This small, special operations unit is attached to the air force. The soldiers in this unit are sometimes dropped deep behind enemy lines to carry out commando raids and other secret missions. Though they are not pilots, they are responsible for one of the most important tasks in the IAF.

It is believed that soldiers from this unit were sent to the Deir ez-Zor region of Syria in the days and weeks before Syria's nuclear reactor was destroyed by Israeli warplanes. They were asked to collect soil samples to make sure the site was what Israel's intelligence community had suspected it was.

They use lasers or electronic devices to hit a structure that will help guide bombs or air-to-ground missiles to the exact correct spot. This is especially useful for small and sensitive targets. It's also a way to limit collateral damage when targets are in heavily populated areas, as the enemy often operates in populated areas. When Israel feels it has no choice but to strike those targets in order to protect its own citizens, the desire to limit civilian casualties on the other side is always strong. World opinion quickly turns against Israel when civilians are harmed.

That former member of Shaldag is far from being the only Talpiot who morphed into a true commando. Several other Talpiot cadets went to special officers' school right after graduating and became platoon leaders-before going on to join the fighting in Lebanon.

The remarkable story of one of those fighters (whose current status and sensitive security position necessitates withholding his name) continues to inspire recruits. I will call him Natan. Friends and soldiers under his command say he's "the salt of the earth." And he looks like the warrior he always wanted to be. His hair is cropped short to the skull. Built like a middleweight champ, his shoulders are big and broad. Not the type of guy you'd dare into a fistfight.

Natan is from a small agricultural town a few miles south of Lebanon. A few miles to the east is the Syrian border. As a child, he practiced safety drills, and he remembers the rocket fire from Lebanon being a little too close for comfort.

Of the generation called "the children of the Yom Kippur War," he was born shortly after the fighting came to an end. At the age of twelve, a doctor told him he'd never reach his dream of becoming a fighter pilot because he had far from perfect eyesight. His mother was terribly disappointed for him, but he happily told her, "Instead of flying planes, I will build planes that don't need pilots." From that point on, without knowing much about Talpiot, he was guiding himself in that direction.

Because he feared recruiters would not find him in his small town, Natan decided to apply to Talpiot, a rarity in those days. As he made his way through the labyrinthine application process, he was intimidated by the "room full of generals" throwing complex questions at him. But it was a kinder, gentler Colonel Avi Poleg who led the interview. The skinny small-town kid, who would later go on to become an important fighter in the IDF, was asked how a microwave works. "I remember having almost no idea, but making up a coherent answer. The rest is pretty much a complete blackout. I was very, very focused, and tried to keep my head up and not look down. I came out with almost no recollection of what happened." He also thought his chances of being accepted were zero.

As Natan started thinking of alternatives, he heard that more than half of his high school class had been accepted into the paratroopers. Resigned that his weak eyesight would preclude him from going into a combat unit, he thought of "doing something else," when the phone rang. He'd been accepted to Talpiot. He was ecstatic!

His Talpiot class was assigned to basic training with the paratroopers, a unit he'd always admired. While not the top student in his class, when it came to military life, he excelled. This cadet thrived on visits to army outposts, naval ships, air force bases, artillery teams in the field, armored units, and research and development teams working on exciting, futuristic projects. "My favorite part of Talpiot was those special sessions when we visited and got training between semesters. I remember coming back home and seeing all my friends who actually went to combat units. I could say 'last month I did your training, this month I did yours.'"

The students in his class were known to be exceptionally eager to question the upper echelon of the Israeli high command.

One day, the class toured an air force base and heard a lecture from General Avihu Ben-Nun, commander of the Israeli Air Force from 1987 to 1992. As a pilot, Ben-Nun became an ace, with at least three confirmed air-to-air combat kills – two Egyptian MiGs and a Russian MiG flying for Egypt. He was revered throughout the country.

The general was explaining his decision to buy more F15s than F16s. The Talpiot class he was addressing had been in the army for less than two years. Natan recalls, "One of the guys raised his hand and actually challenged him: 'That was a terrible decision. How could you do that? Can't you see what the air force really needs?' In the end, Ben-Nun explained why he did what he did, and he clearly won the argument. But in how many countries do twenty-year-olds question the wisdom of legends?" The student-turned-warrior continued with a mischievous smile. "When we met big commanders, it took us no time to ask questions. That was our spirit. Everything was challengeable. I don't know if it was annoying to the commanders and embarrassing to our officers, but as I'm older now, I can see how it would be."

As this exceptional young cadet hit the middle of his second year, he began to have second thoughts about the academic track of Talpiot. He loved being in the field and felt that he might be able to contribute more there. He started toying with the idea of going to field officers' school, with hopes of leading a platoon. His commanders told him they could help him move in that direction, but they urged him to finish his classwork and degree first.

Despite enlisting in Talpiot, Natan never lost his desire to become a true warrior. After graduating, his classmates took their assignments – mostly in research and development – while he hit the dirt, literally. He moved back into basic training, then worked his way into officers' school and commanders' courses.

His aim was for a unit that until recently had been a state secret, an anti-tank missile unit. The missile, called "Tamuz," is a shoulder-fired guided missile developed by Rafael. It can also be fired from a mounted position on a jeep or small armored vehicle. It is propelled with a small amount of solid fuel, making reloading relatively easy.

The Tamuz has been used several times during the Syrian civil war by Israeli troops patrolling the border. When Syrian mortar shells are fired into Israel by the Syrian army or by rebels, on purpose or accidentally, Israel has often responded by destroying the source of that ground fire with the Tamuz missile.

Natan clearly has enjoyed his service in the field and is proud of it. Enthusiastic about the Tamuz, he says, "The missile is guided by a television control. You have a camera at the head of the missile and you just maneuver the missile to the target. For me, it was a great combination of state-of-the-art technology and a field-focused unit."

For more than a dozen years, he was in that same anti-tank unit; a walking, talking, tank killer. If war came, his objective would be to use the element of surprise to take out enemy tanks without the IDF having to deploy full tank units in those areas. Among other things, his unit is trained to open fire on tanks several miles away without being detected or tracked by the enemy.

He's now a lieutenant colonel in the reserves, in charge of up to four hundred men, and he trains his teams to be capable of reloading and firing in fifteen-second intervals. As a reserve officer, he is an anomaly for many reasons, one of which is that he sincerely enjoys his reserve duty. For him, the ideology of service is mandatory. He believes "The reserves are the real green army and need to stay in shape and stay ready. Our reserves have fought for and saved the country in all of Israel's wars. I found my home here in the reserves." He serves seventy to eighty days a year, a very high rate for Israelis. Most serve in the reserves for a few weeks a year, at most.

Military historians agree with his assessment of Israel's reserves. Because the standing army only has approximately 175,000 men and women, the reserves are especially crucial. There are almost four times as many reserves as there are regular soldiers. In the past, the main goal of Israel's standing army, when under attack, was to hold off the enemy until the reserves could get in place. While warfare has changed, as has Israel's army, generals and political leaders know that surprises happen and the reserves are still held in very high regard throughout the country.

This modest Israeli from a small town, who feared he'd have a less than stellar military career, is often asked by Talpiot to come back and lecture to the recruits. Of course, he always says yes. Natan has been instrumental in inspiring more Talpiot graduates to move into the ground forces, and the IDF hopes that still more will follow in his large, capable and dedicated footsteps.

Chapter 15

Israel's New Heroes

*I*srael loves America. They look to the USA as the land of opportunity. They see it as a great place to shop, so much so that Israelis visiting the US bring an empty suitcase for the new clothes they'll buy and bring home. Israel also eats up American television. They love *Seinfeld*, *The Simpsons*, *Sex and the City* – the list goes on and on. One day Assaf Harel, an actor and writer in Israel, was watching an episode of the HBO original series *Entourage*. If you're not familiar with it, the show is about a kid from Queens who makes it huge in Hollywood, becoming a big star. His older step-brother was already a b-list actor, but he also brings his two closest friends to California with him. One becomes his manager, the other runs the homes where the four live together in some of southern California's nicest neighborhoods.

Harel was watching reruns of the show when news came in that Mirabilis, the company behind the instant messaging computer program known as ICQ, had been bought by AOL for $287 million and another $120 million in deferred payments.

It was the most anyone had ever paid for an Israeli company, by far. Israelis were absolutely captivated, and they quickly learned the background of this incredible company and the reason for its great market value. Mirabilis was founded by five Israelis in 1996. Four were friends, the fifth was Yossi Vardi (now a legendary investor in Israel and the father of one of the original four). They decided to come up with instant messaging, after realizing that the technology existed but that nobody was even really experimenting with it. Their goal was to be able to connect computer users using Microsoft's Windows operating system.

Harel says, "When Mirabilis was sold it was a substantial event for the young people of this country, in fact for everyone in Israel. A few guys created something on their own and sold it for hundreds of millions. This had never happened before in Israel. We had never had young millionaires, especially ones creating their own wealth. I remember how enthusiastic everyone in the country was about it. And I thought if all of Israel was so interested in reading about it, they would likely watch a show about it. Since then, this kind of entrepreneurship has happened over and over. But we were the first to really turn it into a popular culture event."

Harel took the story line of the young Israeli millionaires and applied the success factors of the American series. "*Entourage* was a dude series. Dudes walking and talking. ICQ gave us the context for *Entourage*, Israeli style." He and his friends began writing immediately after getting the idea. A few months later, the show was given the green light and they started shooting in 2005. Harel is the idea man for the show, but also one of the stars portraying Guy Fogel, the most serious of the four main characters.

The show is called *Mesudarim*. In English, that title would translate to something like "settled for life." The show is a dramatic comedy about how the four friends live their lives after selling their high-tech company to an American firm for $217 million. The four friends buy a mansion together. They're in each other's business over women, over money and over how they can possibly take the next step together in business. *Mesudarim* quickly became Israel's highest rated comedy series.

Harel is a smart and savvy producer, director, writer and actor. He knows the country very well, and that helped him capture the essence of how Israel was changing. He saw that it was becoming a society that so values entrepreneurship and technology that he could turn a multi-million-dollar technology sale into a TV series. And he astutely realized that the country's heroes had shifted.

"It used to be that Sayeret Matkal (Israel's Special Forces) was the unit that everyone strived to be in," he explains. "They were our heroes. They were the stars: people like Ariel Sharon from Unit 101 in the paratroopers, Ehud Barak and Benjamin Netanyahu, who were both from Sayeret Matkal. They were our special clubs. But now it's the high-tech units that are most revered – 8200, and especially Talpiot. Israelis recognize high-tech players the way Americans recognize athletes and celebrities."

Harel believes the changes in Israeli society were born from the disillusion of the Yom Kippur War in 1973. "Years ago, fighters created an identity for Israel. Everyone went into army service and it used to tell you who you were going to be. But after that war, the nation started to change. We went from an emphasis on brawn to an emphasis on brains. Talpiot and those other "thinking" units represent Israel's global contribution to innovation; brains are the new passport to global society. So now these 8200s and Talpiot graduates are our new heroes."

The battle between brains and brawn, individualism and the common good, soldier and executive, has existed in Israel from the very beginning. For decades, that battle manifested itself in the rivalry between Yitzhak Rabin and Shimon Peres. Many in the world always saw the two Israeli political giants as allies. But everyone in Israel knew otherwise.

"Rabin and Peres hated each other. Rabin was the fighter, the general. Peres was never a soldier, but he was one of Israel's first executives in the Ministry of Defense. Fighters were taught to not trust people who didn't fight, and Peres resented that attitude. There was this everlasting tension between their two different approaches, and they were always up against each other in the Labor party. It was uniforms versus suits."

Assaf Harel sees Talpiot's success in both in the IDF and in Israeli culture as the ultimate win for Peres. "Until recently, Israel was still in the era of the fighter," he affirms. "Now we're moving on." Assaf also believes it won't be long before the soldiers who were in elite technology units like Talpiot will take on political roles in the country, perhaps even the office of prime minister.

Talpiot's success is also evidence of Israel's rotation from a socialist society to a much more capitalistic society. As one who watches Israeli society and culture closely, Assaf's take is that money is now more important than ever in Israel. "But Israel is far from the only country where money is more important than it once was. That's certainly true in the United States and the Western world. That's just the way things are. There's no use in judging it; you just do your best. You could argue that this development is good because it promotes education. People strive to be better educated, they earn higher wages, and donations for charitable causes come from that money." That being said, his next project for Israeli TV is the opposite of *Mesudarim*. It's about old men sitting in a café all day, griping about their lives.

With the changes in societal attitudes comes new popularity for Talpiot recruits. Many members of Talpiot say that after they enlist in the unit, it's amazing how many teenagers from their old neighborhoods and high schools take the time to find their phone numbers. They call them to ask about what they're doing and about their path to Talpiot.

Saar Cohen is from Hadera, just north of Tel Aviv and he's the first student from Hadera High School sent to Talpiot. "Young kids track me down" says Cohen with dismay. "They ask what will happen to me in Talpiot? How do I get in?"

Obviously, they're on to something. They want not only the education, the training and the prestige of the program. They want the added benefit of being able to say for the rest of their lives that they are part of the Talpiot elite. The rewards are many.

CHAPTER 16

"TALPIOTS ONLY NEED APPLY"

Networking is a huge part of the Talpiot experience – for cadets, for graduates in a full time army unit, and especially for those who have moved on to the private workforce. Known casually as "Talpiots," grads hire each other, help each other find jobs and provide a boost whenever possible. After all, it's a network of people born and bred to solve problems, answer questions and unravel life's riddles.

Marina Gandlin will one day soon take part in that Talpiot tradition. For now, she's helping her boyfriend, an alumnus of Unit 8200, look for a start to his career. "We were looking online for jobs for him and we were shocked to see how many of these top jobs in communications and computers say 'Talpiot only,'" she exclaims. "For me, it will help. If your company is looking for a leader, you might take an air force leader or a combat leader. But if you're looking for a leader and a tech specialist, you might well say 'Talpiot only.' It's the best of the brands."

Those "Talpiot only" ads are often published and posted on job sites by non-Talpiot graduates eager to have Talpiots work at their company. But when the company is run by a Talpiot, especially a start-up, the desire to work only with other Talpiot graduates intensifies. Many would say they speak a special language, they truly understand each other, there is a trust from one Talpiot to another, they know how to get things done and they share unique common experiences.

"Talpiot is a great platform for networking because it is such an intimate program," says Elad Ferber, of the twenty-fifth class of Talpiot. "Three years and a few months of eighteen hours a day with the same thirty people, you get to know the boys and girls very well. You literally can tell who they are when you see their shadows. They'll do anything for you. We feel a real obligation to help each other. This is especially true for anyone in your class and for one year above and one year below you. This strong connection lasts during the program, into service and into the private sector. Nothing is off limits. It's a very tight knit community, and while we all need to make a living, money never pops into the equation."

A few of the graduates of this elite club came up with a program called Talpinet. It is an online forum for graduates only. It helps put one grad in touch with another if they're looking for someone to fill a certain role on an executive team, if they need a programmer with certain skills, or if they're just looking to solve a problem previously thought unsolvable.

From Talpinet, air force pilot Arik Czerniak came up with the idea for "Talpimeet." Several times a year, Czerniak finds a venue and invites all seven hundred-plus of the Talpiot graduates to a one-night forum. At each forum there are several speakers, Talpiot graduates who are rising to the top of their fields.

One such forum was held in the spring of 2012 inside a large lecture hall at Tel Aviv University. Graduates from thirty different classes showed up; attendance was in the hundreds. They reunited, reminisced and heard presentations by fellow Talpiots on how a cell works, grows, modifies, can be mutated and cured.

They also heard from Elad Ferber, quoted above. Before he was accepted to Talpiot, Ferber had been dead set on becoming a fighter pilot. He'd already started the recruitment process. But like Arik Czerniak several years before him, he decided that pursuing Talpiot would be a good thing to do as well, so he began the parallel process of applying to both. One of his oddest memories was being asked by the Talpiot interviewers to identify Janis Joplin and Florence Nightingale, and to explain how World War I began. "I knew Janis Joplin," he recalls, "but I didn't know exactly when World War I started or who Florence Nightingale was – but I do now."

Upon finishing his Talpiot studies at Hebrew University, Ferber worked managing programs at the defense contractor Rafael. He believes Rafael was very interested in him for several reasons, including his access to the Talpiot network. "They know that when they bring one of us onto a project, they have access to many more. They know we'll use the Talpiot network. I could attract other Talpiots and access their ideas, even if they don't work on the same projects directly. It's like a beacon for good ideas."

After his stay at Rafael, Ferber moved to the Ministry of Defense where he managed large projects including some that are still very important to the security of the country. His work had to do with a major software upgrade. That project has been deployed and is currently being used by the Israeli army. The rest is classified.

Ferber says it was those types of large projects – where he worked with many people from numerous different backgrounds, representing many interests – that helped prepare him for his future in business. As he finished up his defense work for Israel, he began looking for his first real step in the private world. Passing up a few opportunities presented to him by older Talpiot graduates, Ferber accepted an offer from Stanford University's MBA program. Like most Talpiots who go abroad to study or start a business, Ferber vows to return home.

He sees similarities between his post-graduate program and Talpiot. "Stanford's MBA program is also tight knit and very intense. As in Talpiot, we are greatly encouraged to work together; interpersonal relations are very important. This gives me a second global network."

While studying, he founded Echolabs. The company has devised a way to test blood in a non-invasive way by using electro-optics. Ferber says, "There are a lot of consumer uses for this technology. It is less for the medical community and more for athletes – it tells them how their bodies are behaving under certain conditions, when they should rest, when they should eat and drink. It helps them optimize their bodies."

Ferber constructed the prototype device himself, buying equipment at hardware stores throughout the San Francisco area and putting them on a wearable device the size of a wristwatch. The Talpiot network has been in touch, helping him search for additional funding.

Rotem Eldar was in the sixteenth class of Talpiot and graduated in 1994, nine years before Ferber. Eldar works for Gemini Venture Capital, one of Israel's largest VCs. Eldar was immediately interested in Echolabs. While it's not yet certain if Gemini will make an early stage investment, Eldar has been helpful in putting Ferber in touch with the right advisors who might be able to help with funding now and in the future.

Eldar works on the eleventh floor of a building with a commanding view of the Mediterranean Sea in Herzliyah Pituach, one of the wealthiest towns in all of Israel. There are sushi restaurants on the streets below and an Xbox video-game system in Gemini's lobby. He began working at Gemini in 2011, after helping develop and market a communications company based in Boston. He says the biggest part of his job at Gemini is due diligence, making sure the companies he might recommend for investment would be a good move. He uses the Talpiot network extensively to do this.

Pointing out the window, he offers, "We call this Silicon Wadi. Fifty percent of the startups are in a two- or three-mile radius of where we're standing. Microsoft is a block away. Broadcom is in that building over there. In general, Israel and especially high tech in Israel is like a swamp. Most people know everyone else. But it's my Talpiot network that really helps me get through the clutter and get reliable information faster.

"I know people from Talpiot who have been all over the place in different areas of the military, and their paths have led to different industries and different companies. That network is a huge advantage and time saver to me and to Gemini. From where I stand, you can't tell much from the books or the financials of a company, especially if it's a start-up. What you need is information, and my Talpiot connections get that for me."

Moreover, once Eldar decides that it would be good for Gemini to pour money into a certain project, having Talpiot connections can get Eldar and Gemini in the door. "If it's a good opportunity, it's competitive and difficult. Many VC firms want to invest in good ideas – the next Facebook, if you can recognize it – and everyone wants in. Personal relationships are key. If you know the entrepreneur or someone who knows him or her, you have a better chance of getting in, and getting in first. Let's be honest; there aren't that many great companies to invest in."

When a Talpiot is involved on the other side of the deal, Eldar says with a smile, "We literally speak the same language; we're on the same wavelength; they feel comfortable speaking to me and that gives me an advantage. Talpiot is the kind of network that breaks through boundaries or ignores them."

That sentiment is echoed by five Talpiot graduates who are all employed by Takadu, an Israeli company that monitors urban water supplies and systems. The owner of the firm, Talpiot grad Amir Peleg, brought fellow Talpiots in soon after starting the firm. One of them, Haggai Scolnicov, reflects, "If someone calls me up and the conversation starts with, 'You don't know me...my name is...I'm from Talpiot,' it's immediately a little different. They're not all necessarily people I'd work with. But he probably has something interesting to say. True, there's some element of the old boys' network, but it is generally very helpful. It's a powerful thing. Where else do you consistently have automatic contacts with people ten or fifteen years older or younger than you?"

The precedent for lifelong networking is set during their army years, when Talpiots could ease each other through the bureaucracy. Sometimes politics, bureaucracy, or technical issues would slow down progress, but Talpiots are able to push things forward faster working with Talpiots in other units.

Uri Barkai, another Talpiot Takadu employee, explains,

"Things get lost in communication. In order to talk to another unit, you have to go up the ranks and then back down. So there can be some miscommunication and when you can cut through it by calling a fellow Talpiot, the information flows faster, and that's very good."

Scolnicov recalls an instance when his commander wanted him to take over a communications role. "I said, 'I'm not so sure.' Then I asked, 'Who's on the other side?' When my commander answered, 'Simmy…he's also a Talpiot,' I agreed immediately. Of course, the price a boss will have to pay is that we'll spend thirty minutes a day schmoozing."

Biologist Ron Milo was never much of a chatter. Computer science, physics, technology and chemistry are the tools he uses at the Weizmann Institute, a world class research center in the city of Rehovot, south of Tel Aviv, and just west of Jerusalem. Founded in 1934 by chemist Chaim Weizmann, who would later become Israel's first president, the Institute was rated by *The Scientist* in 2011 as the top place for academics to do research, outside of the United States.

It is a magnet for Talpiots like Milo. The nameplates on the office doors indicate that it is filled with Talpiot graduates. At Weizmann, Milo and his team are working on the "grand challenges of sustainability." That means they're working on improving the efficiency of one of nature's greatest achievements – photosynthesis – to grow food faster where it is needed most, in impoverished parts of the world where many people are starving. He explains his complex research in a nutshell: "We are exploring the possibilities, limits and optimality of carbon metabolism. We hope to understand the fundamentals of its design principles, with the goal of improving our ability to produce food and fuel more efficiently."

Ron is very clear about what led him to this path at Weizmann, a perch from which he literally is trying to save the world. "I am trained scientifically and the training in Talpiot was deep and broad. It helped me master math, physics and computer sciences, and that's really key to who I've become."

While he has great respect for the program itself – from recruitment to army drilling to instruction to graduation – he believes none of it holds a candle to how the recruits drive each other, how the programs' instructors manage the cadets and how past Talpiot graduates impact the trajectory of the careers (and lives) of those who come after them.

"In Talpiot, who you are with and the people you're exposed to is as important, or even more so, than the training itself. You're immersed with interesting and excellent people. You're influenced by your commanders and professors who constantly tell you that you can make a difference. By the time you finish the program, you believe that and expect a great deal of yourself as well." Given that kind of heady environment, Milo believes it is no wonder that once a Talpiot becomes involved in an important, engaging project that he will recruit other Talpiots to join him. There's a natural affinity for similar pursuits. And once again, the network kicks in, ensuring that fellow Talpiots coming on board can be trusted to prove themselves valuable.

Rotem Eldar sums up the Talpiot advantage with these words of caution. "Remember there are no tickets to success in life. You can't just rely on saying 'I'm from Talpiot' and get whatever you want for the rest of your life. But you do have the benefit of bonding with great people and networking with great people. While you're ultimately on your own, you have a sort of built-in, personal advisory staff ready to help you find answers and make decisions."

CHAPTER 17

PROJECT SUCCESS

*I*n the last chapter, we saw how the unique Talpiot network placed many graduates of the program at the forefront of Israeli industry. It's fascinating to track the lives of former Talpiots, watching how their training, education and army experience pay off later in their lives. Talpiots have an impact everywhere they go, and they influence the economy of Israel in unprecedented ways.

In 1993, the Internet was in its infancy. It existed only in a few areas where researchers were experimenting with networks. In some cases, individuals with computers hooked up to phone lines could communicate with each other through a hub with a fax-like connection. One literally heard a fax-like dialing system before a connection could move forward.

Even to people in the high-tech world, the prospect that this small network could one day be the center of global business, banking and marketing was still pure fantasy. But a small team of Israelis saw deep into the future. They saw the value of the

166

Internet; they imagined a world where commercial and banking transactions would be done online as a matter of course. They were way ahead of the game.

Marius Nacht, of Talpiot's second class (whom we met in chapter 6), was working for Optrotech, one of Israel's first companies to be listed on the Nasdaq, when one of the top managers there was allowed to create a separate unit known as GAD. Nacht was invited to work for the new division. The boss was very vague about the details, but Nacht took a leap of faith. "He wouldn't tell me what the project was about because he didn't want to spill the beans," he explains. "But he was brilliant, so I accepted the job offer without knowing what I was going to be working on. After I signed the documents, he told me we would be working on a big, new, sophisticated printer. I was so disappointed with myself: a year or two earlier I was saving Israeli pilots in combat and now I'm working on a printer. I felt so stupid. He wanted me to run the software part of the business which was extremely sophisticated. He said he'd only have five people working there; the rest were outsourced."

Optrotech would later merge with Orbit and then became Orbotech, which still trades on the Nasdaq. The company manufactures, markets and services products for the electronics industry, including circuit boards. It also specializes in a process called automated optical inspection where a camera takes very detailed images of an electronics component and then reports whatever problems may exist with the device.

Nacht admits knowing nothing about software back then. "When I was in Talpiot, there was almost no computer science practice. I didn't even know DOS, and back then it was DOS only." Somehow, he later taught himself UNIX and Macro-S before learning how to program on Apple's OSX, all of which were needed at Optrotech.

Then Nacht ran into a problem trying to write code that would allow a computer to operate the sophisticated laser printer he was working on. He remembers, "Nobody could solve this problem. I was told to call this guy named Gil Shwed. He had served in Unit 8200 and was working as a freelancer for Sun Microsystems in Israel. He hated corporate life and would only work on one project at a time before signing on for a new task. He was a freelancer of freelancers. So I invited him to come help me, and a few days later he showed up. He was sitting in front of the monitor and started typing as I was describing the problem – not even what I wanted to do – just the problem. I kept talking, and he kept working. I shouted, 'Hey, why don't you listen to what I'm trying to tell you?' He didn't even look up; just said 'don't worry, keep talking.'"

Nacht laughs. "As a programmer, Gil is amazing. Even today, nobody can match him. In three hours he solved a problem we had been working on for a month – and our team included a man who had a doctorate and another who had a master's degree in computer science.

"He walked out of Optrotech that afternoon – '*ciao, arrivederci*.' But we stayed in touch. I convinced him to come to work for the company. This was quite a feat. He never took orders from anyone. For him to have a boss and a paycheck was absurd. I'm very proud of being able to convince him to come work for me."

Nacht and Shwed left Optrotech a few months later to work for a New York-based company in Israel that automated warehouse inventory. Their clients included Boeing and Proctor and Gamble. Their storage data was outdated, it was running on a system called VAX and Shwed and Nacht converted it all to UNIX.

According to Nacht, all this time Shwed would say "I have a great idea. The Internet is the next big thing. It will need to be secured." In Shwed's mind was the formula for what would later become known as a firewall, software designed to protect a user from all kinds of outside computer-based attacks.

Nacht admits, "I really had no idea what he was talking about. I didn't know anything about the Internet. Even the concept was hard for me to grasp. But Gil convinced me to quit Optrotech with him saying, 'This is happening *now*; we have to do something.' That's how Check Point started."

Even though Check Point was mostly Shwed's idea, Nacht says he generously offered to split the company 50-50. Nacht understood he was about to be buried in an avalanche of work. He took a few weeks off to go to Jamaica to just think and relax in "paradise." While he was on the island, he got a call from Shwed asking if he would mind bringing on a third man, Shlomo Kramer, a friend of Shwed's from Unit 8200. Even though Nacht didn't know him directly, he agreed. The new split was a third for each man.

While Gil was the main driver behind the new company, Nacht recalls, "He didn't even have a computer. So I gave him my apartment; I had an Intel 386. My bedroom became our office. A short time later, Shlomo's grandmother died. Her apartment became our office and I got my bedroom back." Despite having some seed money, Shwed, Nacht and Kramer agreed they didn't want to hire anyone to help them until they were confident they could start getting customers and sustain themselves without outside funding. After all, if they were to fail, they didn't want to take anyone else down with them. It would have been bad for their reputations in a small country, but even worse, it would have been "bad for their souls." So they did most of the small work, the dirty work, the organizational and secretarial work by themselves.

Once things began to look a little more secure, one of their first hires was a woman named Limor Bakal. Her job was to help the trio organize their thoughts and their schedules, providing whatever support she could. She started up the sales and marketing departments; at that point, everyone did everything at Check Point.

Bakal says, "I didn't even know what the Internet was. It was something special at the time, but it was all very technical and academic. We had to educate ourselves before we could approach a potential customer. First you had to explain that they could use the Internet to do business. Then you could talk about potential problems and our solution. You didn't say to a potential customer, 'Connect and use a firewall.' You had to say, 'This is the Internet.' I remember saying to possible customers, 'Do you have a website?' If they said no, I wouldn't bother with them because they were way behind. But in truth, for a tech company, we were way behind ourselves. The first time they brought in a personal computer, none of us wanted to touch it – we were all scared to death. They'd say something about Microsoft and I would say, 'What the hell is a Microsoft?'"

Bakal recalls Marius Nacht chasing accounts in the United States. "He was traveling all the time. He would work and sleep in his car for months, just like a classic Jewish salesman of old. He'd literally go to companies and knock on the door."

When I told Nacht what Bakal had said, he replied with a smirk, "That sounds like me." On one of Nacht's early calls to a company in the United States, he met a chief technology officer near Boston and the guy said, "There's no need for Internet security, no need at all." The company was the software maker, Lotus. "They laughed me out of the office," says Nacht. They thought no protection would be needed for the Internet, that the net would never be a communication tool for commerce. The first time we went there, the network administrator told me, 'I'm never going to connect to the Internet. I won't need a firewall.' What can you say? There's really no need for a firewall if you're not going to be connected to the Internet. Eventually that guy was kicked out, and the person who replaced him called us. I showed him the product and he was so excited he wanted to deploy it immediately on the gateway to the lotus.com network. I told him, 'Look, why don't you try it on a production network first for a bit, learn the rules and learn how to use it, because if you deploy a wrong set of rules on the firewall you're going to kill your own production."

Another early hire at Check Point was Gil Dagon, a Talpiot graduate from one of the program's first classes. Legend has it that he was equal to a whole team of programmers. Dagon was and still is wholly focused on the things that interest him most. In fact, he gave away many of his early options with Check Point, options worth millions of dollars. "Don't worry," Bakal chuckles, "he still got plenty."

From its humble beginnings, Check Point is now a $12 billion company and one of Israel's biggest, most successful and most respected companies. It is still a global industry leader and the firm holds several key patents, continuing to shape and reshape the face of online security.

To find more Talpiot corporate success stories you don't have to look online. Talpiot graduates have used the Talpiot system for problem solving in numerous other industries.

Talpiot is famous for indoctrinating its cadets in the "systems approach." Instead of taking a limited approach to something, look at *all the factors in the situation from above* and find a way to understand the impact *as a whole* before devising a plan.

Like many before him, Gilad Almogy had envisioned himself as a combat commander and had been very suspicious of Talpiot before becoming part of class number five in 1984. Yet he was an excellent problem solver and did well on tests, sometimes without fully grasping all of the concepts. "Maybe that made me perfect for Talpiot," he quips.

Almogy was already a student of the systems approach even before he became part of Talpiot. But he credits Talpiot with making him a systems approach master. "The way Talpiot taught it gave me a great background. Later, I made a real living doing that kind of thinking."

He dutifully finished his three years of Talpiot classes at Hebrew University, specializing in physics and math, then it was off to combat officers' school. As a brigade platoon commander in Golani, he fought in the first intifada and served for a time in southern Lebanon. While lying cold in the dirt during maneuvers, he'd often look around at his young soldiers and think to himself, "I bet none of these guys have advanced physics and math degrees."

After his military service, Almogy was hired by Orbot, where he perfected a system that finds semiconductor defects completely invisible to the naked eye, saving companies hundreds of millions of dollars. In order to work, semiconductors must be constructed perfectly. There can be no chips or scratches on the small devices. (That's one reason why the people who develop them wear suits similar to what you'd see at a biochemical disaster site.)

"You're looking for possible defects that are a few tenths of a millimeter large," explains Almogy. "It's like being told to find a grain of salt in a football field. By the way, there's grass on the field; ignore that. And you need to know what kind of a grain of salt it is, and you have to be 100 percent sure that it's not pepper."

When Orbot was purchased by Applied Materials (known by its Nasdaq symbol, AMAT) for $110 million in 1996, Almogy moved over to AMAT. He was constantly in demand, rising to the rank of senior vice president, after receiving a doctorate in applied physics from CalTech.

He always wanted to start his own company, but it was hard to escape from the corporate giant. "I can look at a full problem, that's my strength," he reflects. Ultimately, he took a long hard look at his own problem, and found a way to break free from AMAT. He knew that multi-system management would be the key to his success.

Almogy founded the California-based solar energy company Cogenera in 2009, and he was able to coax two other top AMAT executives to come with him. He says making a solar panel is similar to building semiconductors in that every panel must be flawless to achieve maximum efficiency. The company's new technology is taking the world by storm with its unique design for solar panels, and it has been able to attract some big-name investors including Vinod Khosla, one of the most successful venture capitalists in history.

Much of Cogenera's success lies in what Almogy calls "the Ikea approach." All of the raw materials are shipped to his plants for assembly. He doesn't have sole suppliers for any of the materials; that way he never has to put all of his eggs in one basket. His company has won several big contracts in

California, including at Facebook's new headquarters, The Sonoma Wine Company and the Clover Dairy, as well as two very large customers in India.

Talpiot grads also stand at the forefront of several technologies still in the development stage. High on the list are mobile technology and self-driving cars. Talpiot grad Itay Gat, of Talpiot's fifth class, is vice president of production programs at Mobileye. While Israel was fighting terrorism in Gaza during the summer of 2014, Mobileye was becoming a public company, listing on the Nasdaq under the ticker MBLY. On its second day of trading, after its successful initial public offering, the Jerusalem-based company boasted a market cap of $7.6 billion.

Mobileye is almost "a third eye" for your car. It can tell if you're about to bump into the car in front of you, and it will even step on the brake, if the driver reacts too slowly. Mobileye also warns of other collision threats on the road, including other cars and pedestrians, by sounding an alert to quickly motivate the driver to take action.

Mobile strategy is another industry attracting Talpiots. A graduate of the ninth class, Guy Levy-Yurista has degrees in electrical engineering from Tel Aviv University, a PhD from the Weizmann Institute and an MBA from The Wharton School at the University of Pennsylvania. He is the father of five US patents that focus on encoding, detecting unauthorized computer programs and optical pulses.

He has spent his life in research and development, first in the IDF and then in the private sector. Levy-Yurista worked to develop mobile platforms for AOL and security software giant McAfee's mobile protection unit. He was the chief technology officer at a company called AirPatrol, which allows the people behind conferences and other business-to-business platforms to control how invited guests use their mobile devices when around sensitive and proprietary information. It also keeps uninvited intruders from being able to access programs on their smart phones – including the Internet, texting and cameras – while in the vicinity of the conference.

Another Talpiot graduate has had so many corporate successes, his friends nicknamed him "The Idea Machine." And Ariel Maislos's ideas became fabulous moneymakers. After graduating from Talpiot in 1994, Maislos served in an elite research and development unit until 2001. Since leaving Talpiot, he has founded and sold two companies. The first was Passave. The company's mission is to make connectivity better, faster, less expensive and simply more efficient for homes and businesses using video, voice and high speed Internet lines. In 2005, revenue was coming in at a pace of $30 million a year. The company was bought by PMC-Sierra in 2006 for $300 million.

Ariel's other giant success was Anobit, which was able to score sixty-five global patents. He and his co-developers came up with a way to make flash storage devices hold more information. While that technology would be prized by any company in the technology sector, it is most valuable to the mobile device market. After being courted by several big name companies, Anobit was purchased by Apple for $390 million in 2012. Maislos stayed on at Apple for a short time after the sale of his company, but left in a few months later, presumably to start another new company that will sell for hundreds of millions of dollars as well.

Of course, money isn't the world's only measure of success. The name of one early Talpiot graduate has been forever enshrined by music-lovers worldwide. After graduating from Talpiot's course-load at Hebrew University, Meir Sha'ashua used algorithms to develop new radar systems for the IDF. Figuring out a way to use algorithms to improve sound, he co-founded Waves Audio Ltd. in 1992. Their products record, mix and master audio, and are widely used in the music and film industries.

Sha'ashua's company also came up with a way to ease the nerves of millions of soccer fans all over the globe. During the World Cup in 2010, fans at South Africa's stadiums were blowing vuvuzelas, loud horns that make a very distinct buzzing sound. On the opening days of the competition, the BBC alone reportedly received several hundred complaints, all begging the network to do something. FIFA, soccer's governing body, refused to ban vuvuzelas from the matches, so Waves Audio stepped in to provide the solution. They quickly developed and offered a special plug-in to television networks who could use the product to drown out the buzzing.

The company won a Technical Grammy award in 2011. On the red carpet in Los Angeles, Sha'ashua shook off credit for his inventive products, graciously telling interviewers, "It's a great honor! I can only think of the Waves staff – all the employees who actually made this happen."

Chapter 18

Life Savers

We met Eli Mintz, of the fourth Talpiot class, in chapter 3, and the trajectory of his career inspired all who came after him. After his discharge, Eli went to France to study business at INSEAD (one of the largest graduate business schools, with branches in different parts of the world). His wife Liat, a bio-scientist, found a job working at the Pasteur Institute in Paris, a non-profit foundation dedicated to studying biology, diseases, vaccinations and micro-organisms. "In the early nineties, the French were leading even the Americans in researching the human genome," Eli explains. "Of course, the Americans quickly caught up and left the French behind. But at that point, there was a lot of effort in France. We were really in the right place at the right time."

While at INSEAD, he was trying to figure out what to do with his algorithm and business expertise when Liat suddenly had an idea. The two would combine their knowledge to develop a computer that would make genomic data mining faster, more reliable and more effective.

From that idea blossomed Compugen, one of the first companies to use sophisticated algorithms to work on genomic data mining and mapping of the human genome. True to form, he founded it along with a few other Talpiot graduates, Simchon Faigler and Amir Natan. (Later they'd add another Talpiot to the team: Mor Amitai would become a longtime CEO of Compugen and one of Talpiot's brightest business success stories.)

Together they developed a computer that could map and analyze DNA, enabling pharmaceutical researchers at drug companies like Merck, Pfizer, Bayer and Eli Lilly to search genetic codes in order to develop more effective drugs.

But it took the marketing know-how of an American to take Compugen to the next level. Martin Gerstel grew up in the United States without paying much attention to his Jewish heritage. He just wasn't that into it; it didn't seem relevant as he went to Yale, then worked his way up the ladder in California's booming bio-tech industry. He made a real name for himself as CEO of Alza Corporation, a firm that makes drugs that fight everything from AIDS to ADD.

While on a business trip several years into his career, he met a young Israeli woman. She convinced him to visit Israel shortly after meeting and it changed his life forever. He felt at home the instant he got off the airplane, a feeling many non-Israeli Jews describe regarding their first trip to Israel. But Gerstel did something about it. He married that young woman and became a serial backer of great ideas that were popping up in Israel's business community. Among the companies that attracted Gerstel as a financial backer and management consultant, was Compugen.

When Gerstel met Mintz and other Talpiot grads, he was

extremely impressed. "There's nothing like Talpiot anywhere else," he says with enthusiasm. "The people that come out of the program think differently than the typical people coming out of even the top universities anywhere in the world. Just look at how they got this way. The Talpiot program is built on a desire to serve the world and your country. It's such a concentrated effort for nine years. Think about that, nine years when you're only eighteen. They're learning, and they're developing, and applying their knowledge to real problems where the lives of their brother, sister, cousin and parents may depend on whether they're right or wrong. You can always count on the technology here. Marketing? They don't have a clue. But when it comes to technology, Talpiot teaches them to be the best."

Brought in by some of Compugen's bigger investors to "business-fy" the company, Gerstel steered the company through a major transition shortly after Compugen listed and rose on the Nasdaq.

And he immediately realized that Compugen was vastly underpricing the best product on the market. "Their computer was much better than the competition that was selling for $1.2 million. Compugen sold its version for $30,000." Ironically, the high quality of Compugen's computer caused a drop in its sales. "They were so good and so fast nobody needed another one," Gerstel recalls.

He came to firmly believe that Compugen needed to rebrand itself from a computer company to a life-sciences company. Yet his idea to change the focus of the company would soon lead to the exodus of the company's founders.

The original Talpiot team also had a beef with conventional wisdom in corporate circles. As Gerstel led the four – he calls them "kids" – from meeting to meeting with the biggest pharmaceutical companies in the world, it was apparent to him that they were right and everyone else was wrong. "I quickly realized that these kids in the room, the Compugen guys, knew more about biology and the building blocks of life than the rest of the world. We visited with a number of major pharma companies who would say, "You're good mathematicians, but your theories can't be true." They couldn't get away from their central dogma of biology: one gene, one transcript, one protein. So we came back and set up a bio lab to test the predictions we found in our computer. And we found they were correct. Over a number of years, slowly but surely, we transformed ourselves into a life-science company. We hired more biologists; we increased our investment in lab work and research."

In essence, Gerstel and the new wave of Compugen executives put the company on a new track where it had a better opportunity to attract new clients. And that second generation of management was also provided by Talpiot. Gerstel looks back with reverence. "It's the way they think," says Gerstel. "The issue for the Talpiot graduate is to first identify the problem and then get to the bottom of it."

With signature energy, flair and pride, Gerstel says that Israel, (thanks in large part to Talpiot and Compugen) is the world leader in algorithms. "Nobody does it better. And Israel *should* be a center for this. It has the algorithms and the biology, both among the best. Three of the last seven Nobel Prize winners in life sciences have been Israeli. They shouldn't give Nobels in Stockholm, they should give them in Jerusalem or Tel Aviv."

Occasionally Gerstel has been accused of being too enamored with Talpiot, to the point of embarrassing Compugen's executives during sales pitches. One former Compugen executive remembers being especially embarrassed. He would say to his friends, "I travel all over the world and nobody outside of Israel has ever asked me about Talpiot. Even inside Israel it is very rare because people just don't know about it. Martin would give everyone a glowing lecture about Talpiot, and I would have to just sit there, while the pharma execs would stare. It was awful…but he is a good salesman."

While founder Eli Mintz and Martin Gerstel didn't get along well in business, years after their high profile Compugen split they only had praise for each other. Mintz remembers successful seed investor Jonathan Medved putting up money, "but his most important contribution to Compugen was the introduction he gave us to Martin." Mintz continues, "We were so fortunate to meet him. He was really important in making Compugen what it is. Having Martin Gerstel on board was a huge plus because of his business experience, his connections, his ability to raise capital, his strategic sense and his understanding of the biotech community through his experience at Alza. We were really entering into biotech without anyone in the company having experience in biotech. He was a great guide."

When hearing of Mintz's praise, Gerstel was genuinely touched: "I never knew he felt that way."

Just as serendipity brought Gerstel to Israel, a chance occurrence changed the future of Guy Shinar, of Talpiot's eleventh class. Before joining Talpiot, his goal had been to eventually become an air force pilot or a naval commando, and he had hoped to continue in that direction. But during basic training, his eye was hit by shrapnel during a live fire exercise. Told that his vision would be permanently impaired, he abruptly realized that his dreams of combat service were finished.

But he would more than make up for it after a long and difficult road. His first year of Talpiot study at Hebrew University was exceptionally challenging, but eventually he fell in love with science. "I knew it was something I wanted to do for the rest of my life."

After graduating he went on to research and development, in Israel's ordinance corps and then in the intelligence corps. Though he still felt that he was missing out on combat while developing new systems through research and development, he started to realize that the contribution he was making to Israel's defense was important and would be long lasting. "That's life," he reflects, "You choose one thing and give up on the others. There are always pros and cons."

After leaving the army a decade after starting, it was off to business school in France. At this point, Shinar was starting to think more and more about the growing medical device field in Israel. Immediately upon returning to Israel, Shinar became the first person hired by X-Technologies, a company that was formed to develop and sell catheter technology for cardiac patients. It specialized in making angioplasty balloons used by heart surgeons to widen obstructed arteries. A balloon is inserted into the patient and inflated, allowing for better blood flow.

Four years after its founding, X-Technologies was bought by Indianapolis-based Guidant for $60 million in cash, plus another $100 million for hitting set sales markers. Guidant reportedly agreed to aggressively market X-Technologies' product. Three years after the close of the deal Guidant became the buyout target of several major corporate titans including Johnson and Johnson, Boston Scientific and Abbott Labs. In the end, a bid from Boston Scientific aided by Abbott Labs won the long takeover fight.

Despite specific guarantees from Guidant promising to market and promote X-Technologies' products, Guidant instead focused on other ideas, putting X-Technologies on the back burner. Shinar, X-Technologies' founders and top investors sued Guidant for failing to properly market and meet sales goals. In the end, the case was settled, leaving Shinar and his fellow plaintiffs short of the original $160 million sales figure, but still very well off.

At the time, Guidant's buyout of X-Technologies was one of the first sizable purchases of an Israeli medical device company. That deal signaled to the world that Israeli companies and technologies were on the global business stage.

Shinar went on to serve as a board member of several other Israeli medical device companies before co-founding a company called Javelin Medical, where he also serves as chief technology officer. The goal of Javelin is to prevent stroke in high risk populations, specifically patients with atrial fibrillation, a common form of arrhythmia (which involves an irregular rhythm of the heart). Shinar explains, "There are no good treatments for stroke right now, and prevention is the right strategy." Javelin is currently testing its technology on animals and hopes to move to human trials shortly.

Like many Talpiot graduates, Shinar says he was drawn to the medical device field because it requires mastery of various disciplines: technology, medicine, clinical trial design, statistics, quality assurance, as well as regulatory and intellectual property, to name a few. For Talpiots, it's a natural fit. "People who have gone through Talpiot have a genuine competitive advantage in working to solve several problems at once from a variety of different perspectives," Shinar points out. "We were taught to use the systems approach for years, and this is exactly the kind of skill set required in the medical device industry." Shinar credits Talpiot as being the formative event in his life; nothing has had a bigger impact on him.

All that Talpiot creativity and brain power was harnessed by an enterprising Israeli business giant, Yossi Gross. Though his own military service preceded the emergence of Talpiot, his entrepreneurship in medical device technology has attracted a healthy cadre of Talpiot graduates. It is a burgeoning field limited only by the scope of one's imagination.

Gross's personal history includes aerodynamics engineering and a stint as one of the leading engineers on the Israeli Air Force's Lavi fighter jet. He left that position because he felt the bureaucracy of a big project at a huge company was draining him of his creativity. Shortly after that, his wife complained that her electric razor wasn't working properly. Gross went beyond fixing it: he transformed it into a product that eventually became the world's leading brand —"The Lady Remington Smooth and Silky" electric razor.

However, Gross quickly soured on the consumer electronics business. "One month I was developing jets for the Israeli Air Force. The next, I was making ladies' shavers. I went from high tech to low tech. It was frustrating."

He didn't know it then, but he was about to get his chance to move into a groundbreaking area of high tech and to work with some of the best minds in Israel and the world. Soon after separating from Remington, he met another Israeli entrepreneur who had an idea to develop mini-pumps to deliver pharmaceuticals. "I didn't know anything about it at the time, but I told him I could make this." A short time later, he took the idea and his designs to the Irish biotech company, Elan. They invested in the drug pump, giving Gross seed money to develop his own ideas and companies in the new world of biomedical engineering.

Yossi Gross now has six hundred patents to his name and has started more than a dozen companies in biomedical engineering. He groups most of those companies under the name Rainbow Medical, which also serves as a funding arm for the companies and technologies it owns. One of the companies under the Rainbow umbrella specializes in developing minimally invasive implants designed to help hearts work better. Another one of his companies efficiently reduces fat with ultrasound, lessening the need for liposuction procedures which are expensive and require a long recovery period.

Since the beginning, Gross has looked to Talpiot to staff the companies under his control. In Israel's medical device sector, Talpiot graduates have a clear advantage because of their high proficiency in engineering and their ability to incorporate new technologies and new ideas. They're also highly respected because they can understand and manage several different parts of a project at one time – from the mechanics to the technology, to the medical realm, to software production.

The CEO of one of Gross's companies, Nano-Retina, is Ra'anan Gefen, a graduate of the third class of Talpiot. The company is working on a tiny artificial retina to help patients who have lost, or are losing their eyesight, to see well again. Right now, the main candidates for the artificial retina are patients suffering from age-related macular degeneration. Trial tests continue as the product inches toward perfection.

Gefen spent most of his career developing better communications technologies and naval systems for the IDF. After more than two decades, it was time for him to leave. Because he was a creative innovator and had experience managing large, multifaceted projects, many doors opened to him. Looking back, Gefen knows the values that influenced his choice. "I didn't waste a minute during my twenty-three years in the military, and I didn't want to waste my time in the private sector. That was for sure. The work I'm doing here is very meaningful; helping humanity is very important to me."

He gives credit to Talpiot for getting him to a point in life where he could run a company in a field that's still in the start-up stage, a field hungry for new and innovative ideas. "Talpiot shaped who I am today: it taught me how to be innovative and to have the confidence to use that innovative drive."

A California company called "Second Sight Medical Products" has proven that Gefen is on the right track in a growing field. They have a product similar to the artificial retina being developed by Nano-Retina, and it has already been implanted in several patients. Geffen is watching Second Sight's progress very closely. "They are a competitor, but we're rooting for them. They've proven, as we did, that this technology works. It needs to be updated and get better, but it works."

One of Gefen's first hires at Nano-Retina was another Talpiot graduate, Kobi Kaminitz of the sixteenth class. We met him in chapter 12, working on cameras and electro-optics for Israel's satellites. Kaminitz notes that despite the name Nano-Retina, the company isn't quite dealing with nano-technology. The components are incredibly small, but not small enough to be considered nano-technology. Utilizing his experience in the military, the artificial retina he is developing with Gefen uses a lot of the same technology employed on Israel's fleet of intelligence space satellites. "Our goal is to use a chip less than five millimeters large, like chips used in a cellphone's digital camera slot. On one side is the lens; on the other side is a series of pulses that sends signals to the retina. It replicates photo receptors, rods and cones in the human eye," he explains.

Another creative company under Rainbow Medical's umbrella is Maxillent. It specializes in making minimally invasive dental implants; its top product is an innovative way to conduct a sinus lift, a procedure which will increase the amount of bone in the upper jaw area.

Gideon Fostick is the CEO of Maxillent. Fostick's grandfather left Belarus in 1939 as World War II and the Holocaust were just beginning. He remembers his grandfather telling him of the awful pogroms he escaped in Europe. His grandmother was from Poland and lost her entire family in the Holocaust. His family heritage was just one of the reasons that Fostick was so eager to dedicate a decade of his life to Talpiot, the army and his country.

Fostick first heard of Talpiot while he was a high school student in Tel Aviv – and he knew he wanted in. He made it into the tenth class of Talpiot in 1988. After graduating from the academic portion of the program, mastering physics and engineering courses and receiving degrees in both fields, he moved on to a military intelligence technology unit. He quickly became a research and development leader and assisted a section head while working on several advanced military projects that remain largely classified today.

He was awarded one of Israel's highest honors, the Israel Defense Prize for working on multidisciplinary systems. While all the details of the project haven't been unveiled, Fostick's work had to do with advanced alert systems designed to detect the offensive movement of enemy missiles and ground forces. The system combines the use of computer science, physics and electronics to provide the IDF with more warning than ever before of the threat of enemy attacks. His work demonstrates exactly the goal of Talpiot.

Maxillent is growing an average of 15 percent a year, and he credits Talpiot and his intelligence experience for his executive skills. Fostick says both Talpiot and military intelligence taught him to think differently. "Talpiot drills into you, systems approach, systems approach, systems approach."

Apparently that emphasis has never changed. A few years ago, Fostick went back to Talpiot for a reunion, and one of the Talpiot classes at that time performed skits: the punch-line was always "systems approach." Fostick recalls, "In one skit, several students were on the stage acting out a dramatic scene. They went to leave the room and the door got stuck. It seemed jammed, so the first student pulled and banged on the door. Another then tried to force it. A third student looked at the door from all angles, up and down, and side to side, for several minutes. The other two asked him what he was doing. 'Systems approach,' he answered thoughtfully. Then he unlocked the door and it opened easily. Trust me – it was funny."

Fostick calls Given Imaging, an Israeli drug company, a great example of a company using the systems approach. It is most famous for designing a pill with a camera inside that takes pictures of a patient's stomach before exiting the system. "The idea came from a team that worked on guided missiles at Rafael. They know how to make stuff small. They know optics, then they came up with something new. It's a classic example of the systems approach, putting together all of the stuff that we already know and using it for a new purpose."

The late Steve Jobs – who started and ran Apple, of course – wasn't in the IDF and it's likely that he never heard of Talpiot.

But Fostick says, "Jobs may have been the best systems guy in the world. He could always see the big picture, from user interfaces to patents to marketing and public relations. He redefined the music industry almost by himself. He could look at a problem from a wide perspective and create new ideas on how to solve it."

Gideon Fostick points out another common characteristic of Talpiots: genuine admiration for each other's ingenuity and achievements. "There was a brilliant Talpiot graduate from the fifth class. He loved his job, loved research and development, and he was a great help to me in my life and career. He absolutely cherished moments when I figured out something that he could not. We were once working on a project involving optics, and the engineers kept seeing streaks. They couldn't discern why. I finally figured out that it had to do with moisture. It was the happiest I've ever seen him! And that's a large part of what makes the Talpiot community so successful – the desire to help one another and to collaborate, without worrying about who gets the credit."

CHAPTER 19

REUNION!

*I*n the pages of this book, we have met dozens of youthful Talpiot cadets, young men and women whose lives revolved around their experiences in Talpiot and in Israel's military. Educated and confident, they were eager to help Israel progress; and after discharge they were optimistic about their own career prospects. What happened to them? Where are they today?

Imagine a room filled with Talpiot graduates, a reunion of more than two dozen classes. They are seasoned veterans now, and their life stories are varied and colorful. Some will briefly allude to their experiences immediately following their army service or inform us of their current workplace; others will spin long tales of enterprise and adventure.

Talpiot Class 2

We met Opher in chapter 4, when he was tapped by the IDF and the Ministry of Defense to lead Talpiot. It was the first time a Talpiot graduate was selected for the position. Starting with Talpiot's seventh class in 1985, he modeled the program somewhat along the lines of successful Ivy League schools in America, establishing a sense of tradition. He also oversaw an increase in the number of women recruited for Talpiot.

He currently lives in Belgium where he serves as a consultant to European technology companies and teaches at Ghent University, though he plans on returning to live in Israel. Ghent is in a largely Flemish-speaking part of Belgium. His colleagues have pleaded with him to learn the language, but he playfully replies "I already speak one language [Hebrew] of fewer than ten million people; I'd be crazy to learn another."

Talpiot Class 2

Opher was one of the first Talpiot graduates to be given intelligence field assignments. After helping arm the forces in Sinai with sophisticated long-range intelligence devices (1982), he spent time at RCA in Camden, New Jersey. At the time, the company had contracts with the Israel Defense Forces. When he returned to Israel, he was once again a pioneer as one of the first Talpiot graduates to lead new classes of Talpiot cadets. Like his classmate, Opher Yaron, he set a successful example, proving to the army that it was better to use Talpiot graduates as commanding officers of Talpiot cadets.

Talpiot Class 2

When Boaz became a member of the second class of Talpiot, the program was still secret and experimental. After his army service, he went on to a successful career in private industry working in telecommunications. He did a lot of work with Asymmetric Digital Subscriber Lines (ASDL) and other kinds of communications that utilize greater bandwidth to move information quickly.

Talpiot Class 3

A true global adventurer, Gilad has a spot-on nose for business. Not your typical Talpiot, he confides that he was probably one of its most reluctant recruits in the history of the program. When he was being considered for Talpiot, his father, an engineer, told him it was a waste of time: "What the hell are you going to do with physics and math? There's no profession there." Moreover, when Talpiot recruiters told him they would "teach him to think," he laughed at them. Yet by the time Gilad finished his three years of study under Talpiot, he had much greater respect for its methods and goals.

When we last met Gilad in chapter 10, he had joined the navy and became one of Talpiot's first combat officers serving on a missile ship. In his research and development career in the IDF, the bulk of his time was devoted to developing anti-ship radars that helped Israel deceive enemy detection systems.

Gilad used his experience in the navy and Talpiot to have one of the most diverse and dangerous careers of anybody to ever graduate from the program. After spending time working on projects in Japan, he moved back to Israel where he fell in love with a woman running Portugal's commercial office in Israel. At some point, the incessant threat of war and terrorism in Israel was too much for her, and she wanted to move their family of four children to Portugal. Gilad always loved to travel and to experience new cultures, so off they went.

It was a mistake. He found Portugal to be an absolute

mess, with an unfriendly business climate and almost no entrepreneurial spirit, quite the opposite of Israel. He had ideas, but there were so many roadblocks to investing or starting a company, he gave up. He reports, "In Portugal you can't fire anyone. You can't create or innovate. Almost nobody in the country really wants to work. You can't run a country that way and hope to move it forward; it will inevitably fall behind. The economic crisis that exploded in 2009 is evidence of this."

His ticket out of Portugal was his father-in-law's business connection in Africa. The awful, brutal civil war that had ravaged Angola for almost three decades had just come to an end. Angola had been a Portuguese colony for hundreds of years. For better or for worse, those ties created ripe business opportunities.

Gilad's father-in-law wanted to sell Israeli technology to Angola, a country that had very little physical infrastructure and almost no technology infrastructure at all. The Angolans wanted to catch up to the modern world: they needed telephone lines, cellular networks, satellite technology and the Internet. These are all areas where Israel excels.

So in 2004, Gilad moved his family to Cape Town, South Africa. Angola was still far too dangerous a place to move his family. "I was adventurous and hungry, not naïve and stupid," he quips. After setting up his wife and kids in Cape Town, he began making regular trips seventeen hundred miles north to Luanda, Angola. There are several dozen flights a week, making the trip relatively easy, even by western standards. Even though the commute was tolerable, Gilad says, "It was like living in heaven, but working in hell."

One day, he was driving a jeep with his wife outside of Cape Town in what's known as the bush, the unpaved countryside.

They hit a massive bump. "We were three hours outside of town. My wife started screaming at me, but then stopped when she realized I wasn't in the car next to her anymore. I had flipped out head first." He fractured his collarbone and broke ten ribs. It took thirteen hours to get to the hospital. By then, his left lung had collapsed, he suffered a concussion and he was in and out of consciousness. "I was in intensive care for ten days, then laid up in the hospital for three weeks. In order to reinflate a lung, you need to cough a lot. But I had business to do in Angola! I asked the doctor what else I could do. She said, 'Run up and down the stairs over and over.' Everyone in the hospital was soon talking about that crazy Israeli running up and down the stairs with an IV in his arm. But it worked. The doctor said she never saw such a fast recuperation from a collapsed lung. Talpiot and the Israeli army training I had been through taught me the dedication to make this kind of thing happen."

Gilad admits to being a risk taker and says someone who plays it safe would never try to do business in Angola. Crime and security remain problems, and you never know exactly who you are dealing with. "You have to have almost a sixth sense," he winks. Accommodations for business travelers in Angola are far from ideal. "Listen, I'd slept in the dust in Israel for free," he explains. "Certainly I'd sleep in the African dirt – with roaches and Lord knows what else –for millions of dollars. I can't say I loved being there, but the discomfort wasn't enough to stop me."

Industriously, he imported and sold Internet capacity and storage solutions. "Growth was in the double digits," he recalls. "But there was a lot of corruption and a lot of misery there. It's heartbreaking. In the end, I was a middleman selling everything from copper wire to network appliances to data storage systems.

I did not like it, not even for a moment, but I never really felt that I was in danger. I happily left Angola for good."

Working under nearly impossible conditions prepared him for another tough money mission several years later. While Gilad would neither confirm nor deny it, he reportedly was inches from securing a deal with Muammar al-Gaddafi to build resorts in Libya, a short time after Libya reached an agreement with the West to give up its weapons of mass destruction. The deal never quite materialized, and the Libyan leader was violently deposed and killed in the "Arab Spring" of 2011.

After working briefly for the Israeli defense firm Elbit, he attended the French business school, INSEAD. That prepared him to do what he is most suited for: Gilad is now a matchmaker for private and corporate investors looking to pair up with good ideas and good companies. He calls himself "a cross between an investment banker and a scout. I can look at material, analyze it and quickly decide if there is quality and value there. That's what I'm best at." He works for himself – but his Talpiot- and INSEAD-filled address book is what brings him business, new ideas and new connections. He never pitches a deal that he wouldn't personally invest in. "In my business, your name is everything."

Gilad has also joined with several other Talpiot grads to form OTM Technologies, a company at the forefront of making devices that allow a user to write notes or messages by hand on mobile phones and pads. His device is called "the feather."

Talpiot Class 5

Amir's work was primarily in Israel's burgeoning unmanned aerial vehicle (UAV) program in the late 1980s and early '90s. Israel is now a world leader in

UAV and UAV component exports. His work with the program through Talpiot laid the groundwork for that.

He went on to become a serial entrepreneur, founding three firms including YaData, which he sold to Microsoft. He founded and is currently the CEO of a water security company named Takadu (described in chapter 16), based in the industrial town of Yehud. The firm has clients all over the world including municipal water systems in London, Chile and Israel.

Talpiot Class 6

An Israeli Ministry of Defense legend, Eviatar was later known as "the right hand of Talpiot." He was the founder of Nachshon, a high school program that has furnished Talpiot with several cadets. Currently, Eviatar is Israel's top commander on cyber-defense, reporting directly to Prime Minister Benjamin Netanyahu.

Talpiot Class 6

We met Tzvika in chapter 11 as the gutsy young man working for the Israeli Air Force inside Elisra, a defense company where he worked with engineers many years his senior. After leaving the service, he went on to work for two successful start-ups founded by Talpiot grads. He currently works at Amir Peleg's Takadu, along with other Talpiot graduates Haggai Scolnicov, Barak Peleg and Uri Barkai. His work involves designing and testing the system that tracks urban water flow.

Talpiot Class 10

As a youngster living in Japan, Matan developed revolutionary software that enables instant financial transactions from one end of the world to the other. After Talpiot and army service, he took a different route than most graduates. He went to Hollywood.

Matan uses the mathematical software development skills he learned in an elite military intelligence unit to produce a website called audish.com, essentially an online casting agent. Its goal is simple: match directors and film producers with actors and actresses online, eliminating some of the middlemen. When Matan isn't developing the site, he is the managing director of a boutique angel capital venture firm called Secent LLC in Santa Monica. Secent describes itself as providing a "global gateway to early-stage companies who have innovative technologies with great potential to generate revenue worldwide." In other words, he says, "we like to help people make their dreams realities, and we know people who know people."

Talpiot Class 13

Ophir found his niche in Unit 8200, developing software to retrieve data stored in the Israeli military machines' computer servers. After 8200, he founded a company called CloudShare that did similar things for major corporate customers all over the world. He explains that the servers are based in Miami, "because, God forbid, if they'd be based in Israel, you'd never be able to attract clients. What could you say? 'Don't worry, your data is safe even though it's within easy missile range of Syria, Hezbollah, Hamas, Iran and a whole range of terrorists.'"

From there, it was on to Check Point and then to EMC, one of the world's leading companies in information infrastructure solutions. His latest job change took him to Google in Mountain

View, California. He hopes to return to Israel in the next few years.

Talpiot Class 14

Ofir served in a technology unit in the IDF and later became one of Talpiot's wealthiest graduates. Along with fellow classmates, he developed XIV (named after their famous Class 14 of Talpiot), a high-end data storage system that caught the eye of executives at IBM; then it caught their checkbook. IBM bought XIV for $300 million in 2008. At the time, it was the largest acquisition ever of an Israeli company.

Talpiot Class 14

Barak is a rarity among secular Israelis. He grew up in Jerusalem's old city. His family had moved there after the 1967 Six-Day War, for they considered it their patriotic duty to live in areas were Jews were once forced out. Coincidentally, when he was fifteen he moved to Jerusalem's Talpiot neighborhood, a part of West Jerusalem that is more modern than the old city.

Instead of going for the big money after his army service, Barak joined Israel's national police force. He sees crime and corruption – and the lack of respect for the country's laws and institutions – as the biggest threat the nation faces; bigger than Israel's external enemies, bigger than the threat from Iran.

Barak didn't become a beat cop or a traffic officer. His goal was to come up with software that would modernize Israel's outdated way of keeping records. He spent five years working in the police force, updating systems to make the Israeli police more efficient. And his legacy lives on. Since leaving the force, two other Talpiot graduates signed on to add to the effort he began.

Talpiot Class 15

Saar never wanted to use his Talpiot background to make millions. Instead, his goal was to make a significant contribution, even if it meant being in a smaller environment. He turned down a super-lucrative job offer at Check Point, saying the company was just too big for him. Efforts of the Talpiot network to recruit him failed until Saar accepted an offer at EMC in Beer Sheva. He has been a key player in developing EMC's Recover Point, a program that finds lost data after disasters, or massive hardware and software malfunctions.

Talpiot Class 15

We met Arik as the Talpiot grad who wanted to be a pilot at all costs, and left him playing an active role in the reserves, training pilots in dogfighting. After leaving the army, he started Metacafe, an early video-sharing website. In essence, it's a higher quality version of YouTube, with professionally produced videos and Internet-based television shows. He was able to secure $3 million in financing from two of the biggest names in Silicon Valley venture capital, Accel Partners and Benchmark. Arik sold his stake for $2.5 million.

These days, he looks out at the bright blue Mediterranean from his eleventh-floor office in a building that houses the second company he created, Supersonic Ads. The view is stunning, his office is casual; it's the office you might expect for a highly educated fighter pilot turned Internet executive. There's a large model of the anatomy of a Great White Shark, an electric guitar, a few pairs of jeans and sneakers thrown about the room, a heavy green coat and the national jersey of the US soccer team. Supersonic Ads is a global leader in online video game advertising, social networks and direct response advertising. The company also monetizes virtual currency. It is a key component in Facebook's ever-popular Farmville game. Anytime you want to buy something for your use in the game, you go through Supersonic Ads to turn your real money into Farmville dollars. The company's ads hit 500 million social gamers throughout the world.

In his spare time – of which there isn't much – Arik found a way to creatively organize several Talpiot alumni events each year. Graduates give speeches to their fellow Talpiots about the new technologies they've developed and are working on in the private sector. The grads use it as a continuing education series.

Talpiot Class 16

One of several unofficial Talpiot historians, Amir is one of Talpiot's most popular graduates. After Talpiot, he tried to be a fighter pilot, but didn't quite make the cut. Invited to helicopter pilot training school, he declined, saying, "No offense to my many friends who are chopper pilots, but for me it was fighter pilot or bust."

After completing eleven years of service in the army's research and development unit and serving as a Talpiot commander, he was accepted to business school at Harvard, Wharton, MIT, Columbia and INSEAD. He chose the Paris-based INSEAD, fearing that the American schools led down only one path – to American corporate institutions. Amir didn't want to live abroad; he wanted to help develop business in Israel.

Work as a consultant at McKinsey & Company, was followed by a position at Israel's biggest bank, Bank Hapoalim, as the direct assistant to the CEO, the equivalent of a corporate chief of staff. Amir then took his banking experience to the world of global e-commerce, founding "Global E," designed to make international banking easier and more efficient than ever before.

Talpiot Class 18

Argentinian-born Adam served in a technology unit of the Israel Intelligence Corps after graduating from Talpiot. After nine years as a software warrior for the Israeli army, he took his skills into the private sector.

After creating software designed to make personal mobile devices compatible with all platforms at work, saving companies billions in hardware costs, he started work at a new company called Screenovate. Intel is an early financial backer; tech powerhouses Nvidia and Samsung have also signed on to cooperate. Screenovate allows any smart phone to turn your TV into a smart TV. Screenovate users can take whatever is on their mobile device and put it on a big screen television with a simple click. It's great for work presentations, where you can program or save a presentation on your phone, then put it on a big screen for all to see in a meeting. The company is also marketing products for auto companies for dashboard displays, for gaming companies, and for home entertainment. Kariv also used his programming skills to come up with the Public Knowledge Workshop, a free online database that allows the Israeli public to see exactly where the government is spending money, among other important facts and figures about the Knesset, Israel's parliament.

Talpiot Class 26

One of the few women to be recruited to her Talpiot class, Marina's army training was in the especially intense unit of the Givati Brigade. After her basic Talpiot training and education (primarily in physics, math and computer science), she spent a good deal of time on the Ofek satellite project.

While working in research and development, she also became a big part of the Talpiot recruiting system. Today she travels internationally, speaking to women's groups on the importance of women in the Israeli Defense Forces and about gender equality in the IDF.

Though not a Talpiot grad, General Ben-Israel was featured in chapter 7 as an award-winning Talpiot role model. From high-level positions in the intelligence and weapons development units of the IAF, he went on to leadership of MAFAT and took charge of Talpiot. Beyond his military achievements, he has also become a highly valued asset to Israel's business community. He is a former member of the board of directors at Israeli Aerospace and Industries, the country's biggest and most prolific defense contractor (and a leader in Israel's unmanned drone projects). Ben Israel also served on the advisory board at Teva, the world's largest maker of generic pharmaceuticals. Teva and IAI are Israel's two biggest employers. Active in the Kadima party of Ariel Sharon and Ehud Olmert, the general was a member of the seventeenth Knesset (Israeli parliament).

But there is yet another Talpiot graduate at this reunion whom we have not met before. Tall and thin, Yossi Azar looks nothing like a warrior. He looks every bit like a winner of the "Math Olympics" (first prize in London) and the head of Tel Aviv University's prestigious Department of Computer Science.

Recruited to the third class of Talpiot in 1981, Yossi was not a typical soldier – not even a typical Talpiot soldier. By nature bookish and reserved, he says, "Talpiot changed my personality. You learn to belong to a group, and it's a great feeling. I became much more team oriented."

He wasn't quite ready for the rigors of basic training. Because he suffered from asthma, the IDF screening doctors sent him to a less intense training course than the one other Talpiots had to endure. With a wide smile, Azar explains how he beat the system. "I sought out a medical committee and pleaded with them to take me off the asthma list so I could do a regular basic training. Looking back on it all thirty years later, it isn't so easy to understand why I did it. But I was eighteen and very motivated to be part of the group. The other guys thought I was crazy to ask for the tougher training. It was very hard for me, but I made it through."

According to the professor, in Talpiot's eyes Israel had enough fighters and enough academics and engineers. "What they needed was people like us who could straddle both worlds, understand both worlds and connect both worlds."

He notes that the IDF was becoming increasingly compartmentalized. Talpiot's founders were among the first to see this trend and realized the importance of grooming the right leadership for it. At eighteen, he didn't understand the need for this, but looking back on it, he says, "I was wrong.

The IDF was way ahead of me. Talpiot was able to become a new and necessary leader in that new structure." Yet even as he was graduating from the program there were still some detractors high in the IDF brass who would say the program was too expensive and wasn't necessary.

Upon graduation, Yossi was assigned to an intelligence unit. Using math and computers to solve problems was his goal from the start. "I always felt it was important work that I was doing, even though it was academic work," he attests. Even twenty-five years later, he still wouldn't talk about most of the work he did for the unit.

He met his future wife in that same intelligence unit. The two later moved to California where Yossi studied at Stanford before moving to Redmond, Washington to work on various projects for Microsoft. It was there that he met many Iranian software engineers. The experience shot a chill up his spine. He saw first-hand how bright the Iranian scientists are, and though many were anti-regime, some were not. He knew then that superior brain power would lead to a more powerful Iran in the future. "Not such a great thing for Israel or for the free world," he adds thoughtfully.

And that is just one of the reasons Israel needs the edge provided by Talpiot. Yossi is certain that the program is critically important to combat such threats, to fuel the economy and to keep Israel ahead of the technological game. "The program gets motivated people and makes them even more motivated; and that's great for all sectors of Israel. Just look at the special qualities of the graduates. They succeed in the military and then go on to excellent places in academia, industry, start-ups, big companies, small companies – and some stay in the IDF. This is all good for the country."

Chapter *20*

The Future

The future, even the near future, in Israel is never clear. Politics change; while the right and center right have been dominant for more than a decade, shifts in Israeli politics are inevitable. Peace talks with the Palestinians and the greater Arab world come and go. Even with the most savvy analysis, the impact of the Arab Spring – as well as new explosive upheavals, including ISIS – in the Middle East is unpredictable. Israel's relationships with the rest of the world are constantly swinging up and down.

Internally, there are budget problems as well. In 2013, the IDF was forced to lay off hundreds of army careerists. Former chief of staff Benny Gantz, whose term came to an end in February 2015, assigned 250 people the task of finding ways to save money, as the IDF was running a 20 billion shekel deficit. In 2017, a foreign aid agreement with the United States comes to an end. And that deadline is getting closer during an era of changing foreign policy priorities in American politics. While US law says the United States must help Israel maintain a qualitative military edge over its neighbors (the Naval Vessel Transfer Act HR 7177 of the 110th Congress, and others), when it comes to spending bills in Congress, nothing is guaranteed anymore.

The current leadership of Israel's Ministry of Defense, Moshe Ya'alon, a former chief of staff, clearly understands the challenges. In a speech in 2013, he emphasized the need to maintain a massive technological edge over other nations in the Middle East, saying priority must be given to precision firepower, unmanned aircraft and other unmanned defense systems, intelligence capabilities and cyber-warfare.

Efficiency is a key component to keeping Israel safe – efficiency in manpower, expenditures, advanced education and technological deployments. Fortunately for Israel, efficiency isn't an area where the Arabs excel. Third class Talpiot graduate, MAFAT consultant and bio-science executive Dror Ofer says, "The Arabs around us are declining.... We have the upper hand in efficiency." He explains this statement with an equation, as perhaps only a Talpiot-trained bio-scientist/military expert would: "Imagine all Arab armies were very efficient, running at 80 percent of optimal. Since the maximum efficiency is 100 percent – even if our army reached that, we would be only 1.25 (=100/80) times more productive than they per soldier. Since their numerical advantage over us is much greater than 1.25, they could easily beat us with an army twice as large as ours. Now, imagine Arab armies are extremely inefficient, running at 1 percent efficiency. If our army is 10 percent efficient, it is still very inefficient per soldier, but ten times better than the Arabs – thus our upper hand." He adds wryly, "If we were surrounded by 300 million Swiss, we'd be in big trouble."

Just a few years ago, in a bid to increase efficiency and

to emphasize the importance of military technology, the IDF changed the designation of soldiers using computers to bring down enemy infrastructure to "combat soldier." A good deal of speculation erupted in the Israeli media, and an article in the *Jerusalem Post* surmised that the designation was an admission "that Israeli cyber units are used for attack purposes and not only defensive purposes." The IDF had no comment.

The glue that sticks together all of these unique resources for the IDF is Talpiot, though the expense of the program is always under scrutiny. Arik Czerniak, (part time fighter pilot and full time high-tech entrepreneur) discussed the relatively small investment the IDF is making in Talpiot cadets, in return for significant gain. "Talpiot is absolutely necessary for the future. What is the army doing? Paying for thirty or forty kids to go through academic training? It's negligible. They're building a team of people who are really committed to research and development. One air force pilot burns more money in a week than the entire Talpiot program costs for a year. So I don't see it as an expensive program. It's cheap, but structured in a very smart way, making the return on investment very high."

On what future projects will Talpiot grads likely be utilized? They will certainly be expected to work formally and more closely with the Combat Intelligence Corps. It's composed of three different battalions including the Shahaf (Seagull) which works with the northern command, the Nesher (Eagle) in the very busy south with its border at Gaza, and the Nitzan (Blossom) in the central part of the country, which includes the West Bank. These units work with complex new technologies designed to monitor and intercept communications of the enemy without putting soldiers in harm's way. Closed-circuit television cameras are designed to alert troops on the ground when suspected terrorists, or anyone else, is nearing the border or designated de-militarized zones. These technologies are especially valuable to Israel because the IDF no longer needs troops in these danger zones patrolling the border. In the past, soldiers on the border have been sitting ducks for terrorists. Now those soldiers can respond to alerts given to them by the Combat Intelligence Corps while waiting in relative safety.

The commander of the Nesher unit told the *Jerusalem Post* in 2013, "We're known as Gaza's big brother. We see everything. We're seeing Hamas getting stronger and preparing itself. We see them watching us."

During the war in Gaza in the summer of 2014, known in Israel as Solid Rock (and abroad as Operation Protective Edge), Hamas utilized a new offensive weapon: tunnels. It was a weapon the terrorists had employed before, using their underground network in the 2006 attack that led to the capture of Gilad Schalit and left two Israelis dead. But in 2014, Hamas began using these tunnels as a larger part of their strategy. Many Israeli military analysts commented Israel had the advantage in the air, at sea and on the ground, but not underground. Another joked, "Israel should hire Hamas to build the Tel Aviv subway."

But those tunnels were certainly no joking matter. Some stretched from Gaza deep into Israeli territory, surfacing near kibbutzim and other civilian infrastructure. Israeli intelligence discovered that the tunnels were meant to be used during the fall of 2014 in "a mega terror attack" around the Jewish holidays. Inside one captured tunnel, Israeli forces discovered tranquilizers and handcuffs that would have been used to bring Israelis back into Gaza as hostages.

Despite Israel's knowledge of the tunnels, not enough was done to defend against them in 2014. Hamas used them to successfully carry out several attacks in Gaza and inside Israel proper, resulting in the deaths of several Israeli soldiers.

As the war was raging fifty-three miles to the southwest of Jerusalem, the Knesset's Science and Technology Committee finally began looking for ways to combat the tunnel threat. The head of the committee, Moshe Gafni of the Degel HaTorah party, called for the committee to address the tunnel threat immediately after the conclusion of the 2014 war, saying they expect to hear testimony and ideas from experts with experience in geology, mining and other similar fields.

Talpiot also began working on solutions. The tunnel threat is likely to be the focus of future second-year student projects that will be presented to senior army officers. While it's impossible to say what a future solution will look like, everyone agrees that for life to continue with some semblance of safety and security, especially in Israel's southern towns, something must be done. Ideas have already surfaced regarding underground warning sensors, but nothing concrete has been decided.

Avi Isaacharoff, a reporter and analyst for *The Times of Israel* and Walla.co.il (one of Israel's top Internet portals) and author of the book *34 Days* about the Second Lebanon War, surmised in a *Times of Israel* article (August 2014), "Hezbollah was the first to use defensive tunnels to attack IDF soldiers and to continue firing rockets. One can assume that, in the eight years since the Second Lebanon War, Hezbollah has accelerated its digging project on two levels: defensive tunnels within Lebanon and attack tunnels into Israel. Eight years of work can mean that, in the next war, we will find Hezbollah fighters emerging from tunnels deep inside Israel, not necessarily near the border. Yes, the ground there is harder to excavate compared to that of Gaza, but it can be assumed that, as always, what Hamas does well, Hezbollah does better."

It's clear that without a solution from Talpiot or somewhere else, the frightening prospect of more tunnel attacks in the south and or the north could end in tragedy for Israel. In many regards, a technical solution is only the first step for Israel in dealing with the tunnel threat. In a news conference (August 6, 2014), after a three-day cease-fire with Hamas went into effect, Prime Minister Netanyahu dedicated much of his address to the nation and the world media to that tunnel threat: "Israel is working to create technological means to locate new tunnels that will reach into our territory."

Talpiot-trained soldiers also used their technology know-how to construct dozens of remote controlled guns stationed on the Israel-Gaza border that are operated from a command post several miles away, often by specially trained female troops. These guns also help cut back on the number of ground troops Israel needs to make sure that terrorists don't cross the line.

While border battles are certainly a priority, so is longer range fighting. Talpiot graduates are involved in preparing the Israeli Air Force for American made F35s, which will replace the older F16s. One major tool F35 pilots will possess is the helmet display system designed by the Israeli firm, Elbit Systems. Elbit and its staff of Talpiot engineers are working with the US defense firm Rockwell Collins on the project. The fighter pilot helmet of the future gives a flier pictures from on-board cameras giving him a better look at targets, objectives and obstacles, as well as the mechanics and performance of the airplane.

Famous Talpiot graduate and head of MAFAT Ophir Shoham is investing more and more in robotics. He doesn't believe robots will ever replace soldiers in the Israel Defense

Forces. But he is convinced that by 2020 robots will have more combat roles and will cut down on Israeli casualties by going first into hostile territory. He told *Haaretz* correspondent Amos Harel in 2012, "More robots will not replace warriors.... But unmanned vehicles on the ground will go to high-risk targets, you can send them from afar into enemy territory, a kind of front guard, vehicles that watch a situation and shoot. This will happen in the foreseeable future." Shoham envisions a greater presence of robotics on the ground, unmanned ground vehicles (UGVs) almost equal in a sense to Israel's world-class fleet of unmanned aerial vehicles.

The head of MAFAT's robotics division is Lieutenant Colonel Gabi Dobresco. He says many UGVs are already in operation; several are helping with surveillance along the Gaza border, others are aiding troops near Arab areas of the West Bank. He believes UGVs will be used more in the future to find and detonate roadside bombs and landmines. They'll also be used in urban areas to draw fire, helping the IDF locate the enemy. In a release issued by the Ministry of Defense, Lieutenant Colonel Dobresco said, "Robots sometimes go in front of the forces to open challenging roads such as narrow alleys and assist logistically. A robot can help lighten a soldier's burden, so that if the soldier is confronted with a battle, he or she can respond appropriately." He also said that in the future, "the UGV will be equipped with obstacle detection sensors, cameras and other tools, and it will be able to identify the barriers by itself and circumvent them." Talpiots are also at the forefront of technology when it comes to the development of both air- and ground-based remote-controlled fighting vehicles.

Talpiot graduates will also continue to have a major impact beyond the IDF, especially when it comes to taking the Israeli economy to new heights. During a trip to Jerusalem in the summer of 2013, Cisco's CEO John Chambers said that Israel will be the world's first digital nation. Israeli innovators and entrepreneurs, including many Talpiot graduates who are either building the networks or helping to fund them, are connecting more and more sectors of the economy to fiber optics. It will have an impact on the healthcare system, the economy, and how people at home communicate, learn and do business.

One area where Talpiot students have not yet had an impact is in the world of politics. To date, not a single Talpiot graduate has made waves in Israel's political system, but that may one day change. Every Talpiot cares deeply for the country and it's likely that just as they've changed the military establishment, a Talpiot graduate may very well change the political landscape as well.

Though Iran continually threatens "Israel will be wiped off the map," few of the Talpiot graduates interviewed for this book believe Iran is Israel's biggest problem. Colonel Avi Poleg, who turned his army and Talpiot experience into a career in global private education, laughed when asked about the rising power of Iran. He says, "Iran is not a military problem for Israel right now. I'm not worried about Iran's bomb or the Palestinians. The most fearful, problematic thing to me, is the process going on in our society. We stood against very severe challenges in our history because we were strong from the inside. If you see cracks in the internal workings of a society, this is most dangerous."

One of the "cracks" he is alluding to is the rift between the growing Haredi population and general society. Popular resentment boils over into bitter acrimony in the press because Haredim have been exempt from military service since 1948 (when their numbers were comparatively few). Hot debate over their proposed induction into the army only widens the cultural divide, weakening the unity of the nation. Talpiots are also more worried about an unbalanced economy, as well as internal Israeli crime and corruption than they are about an Iranian nuclear bomb.

But societal concerns don't grab headlines the way military threats do. Barak Ben-Eliezer, told *The Marker*, "Education and social issues are perhaps less photogenic, but just as acute of a problem as security. They are internal bleeding issues, rather than external bleeding, and therefore it is more difficult to catch them and expose them."

His allusion to education as another of the "cracks" threatening Israel is surprising. But Israeli education isn't what it once was. In a recent study of teenagers in sixty-five "developed" countries, Israel ranked 41st, alongside Croatia and Greece in mathematics. In science, Israel also ranked just 41st. If there are two areas where Israel simply can't afford to fall behind, it's mathematics and science. Both are critical to a country that prides itself on innovation – and it needs innovation to survive.

Perhaps a Talpiot-like approach is needed to fix the education system in Israel. It's a method already championed by Colonel Poleg, who uses Talpiot as a model when he consults in schools both within and outside of Israel.

David Kutasov, a mild-mannered, soft-spoken string theory physicist at the University of Chicago, describes his job by asking, "Did you ever watch the TV show *The Big Bang Theory*? I have the same job as Sheldon Cooper, the weird skinny guy. My job is to find out how the universe came into being."

Kutasov believes Talpiot will continue to lead in research.

And he knows why. "Research through Talpiot is often about originality. I would not have been as good of a researcher or a physicist without Talpiot. It empowers you.

"A lot of kids I see these days – even at top American universities – are too conventional and not original. At Talpiot, they beat it out of you and push you toward originality. Now let's look at the American system. My daughter was admitted to MIT for engineering. But of her class, only she wants to be an engineer. The rest want to get their MBA, but they stayed with the herd and applied to MIT. Another example: in Manhattan you need the right preschool to get to Dalton, to get to Harvard, to get to the right law school. The system breeds unoriginal professionals, and it only gets you so far.

"It seems the most important tech leaders in the US didn't finish college at all. Steve Jobs dropped out. Bill Gates dropped out. Look at all these MBAs betting on credit default swaps. Didn't anyone ask 'Is this a good idea?' The system breeds followers and not leaders.

"On the other hand, Talpiot consistently breeds leaders. Talpiot emphasizes originality. They bring in people to tell you about what's going on in some branch of the army, then ask you how you would do it differently. They keep challenging you all the time. It's in the genes of the program."

From Talpiot's inception, those "genes" have propelled the program and its graduates to unexpected and unprecedented breakthroughs. One day, these young men and women will undoubtedly start to influence Israel's government and policies, and perhaps even to enhance prospects for peace. As Talpiot alumni expand their influence in all sectors – from education to defense, to the halls of power in Jerusalem – there is hope that Israel will be safe and secure for many generations to come.

APPENDIX

TIMELINE

DATE	HISTORICAL EVENT	TALPIOT EVENT	TALPIOT GRADS' ACHIEVEMENTS
1918/1919	End of World War I. End of Ottoman rule in Palestine. League of Nations grants mandate to Great Britain to rule Palestine.		
1924		Felix Dothan born in Yugoslavia.	
1927		Shaul Yatziv born in British Mandate Palestine.	
November 29, 1947	United Nations agrees to partition Palestine between Arabs and Jews.		
May 14, 1948	State of Israel established. US recognizes Israel.		
1948–1949	Israel is attacked by surrounding Arab nations. War of Independence ends in armistice agreements with Egypt, Jordan, Syria and Lebanon. Jerusalem is divided between Israel and Jordan.		

DATE	HISTORICAL EVENT	TALPIOT EVENT	TALPIOT GRADS' ACHIEVEMENTS
October 1956	Sinai Campaign: Israel takes Sinai with British and French support. Sinai returned to Egypt under pressure from the UN, US and USSR.		
1950s /1960s	Ongoing Arab guerrilla attacks; IDF reprisal operations.		
June 1967	Six-Day War. Egypt blocks the Straits of Tiran. Israel captures Sinai from Egypt; the West Bank, including Jerusalem, from Jordan; and the Golan Heights from Syria.		
November 1967	United Nations Resolution 242 adopted as a framework for peace.		
1967–1970	Egypt/Israel War of Attrition.		
October 1973	Yom Kippur War. Israel is attacked by Egypt and Syria; sustains initial losses but ultimately defeats Egypt and Syria. Cease-fire declared.		
April 1974	Interim report of the Agranat Commission investigating the Yom Kippur War fiasco cites a lack of military and intelligence preparedness. Resignations of several top military leaders, as well as Prime Minister Golda Meir.		

DATE	HISTORICAL EVENT	TALPIOT EVENT	TALPIOT GRADS' ACHIEVEMENTS
November 1974		Professors Shaul Yatziv and Felix Dothan formulate a document titled "A Proposal for Establishing an Institute for the Development of New Weapons." Today it is simply called "The Initiation Document" of the Talpiot program. Dothan and Yatziv's original proposal was to grant degrees in physics and math to gifted recruits within a span of twelve months, and afterwards direct them to creating solutions for the army.	
1974	Intel opens Israel office, its first development office outside of the United States.		
July 1975		A meeting at the Ministry of Defense considers the creation of the Talpiot program. At the end of the meeting, the participants agree it is a good idea, but several questions remain and there is no formal approval.	
1971–1982	PLO is expelled from Jordan in 1971 and sets up base in southern Lebanon. It stages attacks on Galilee residents and is countered by IDF retaliations.		

DATE	HISTORICAL EVENT	TALPIOT EVENT	TALPIOT GRADS' ACHIEVEMENTS
March 1978	Operation Litani. Israel invades Lebanon on a large scale for the first time. The PLO withdraws from southern Lebanon and sets up base north of the Litani River. A UN buffer zone is established on the Israel-Lebanon border.		
September 1978	Camp David Accords are signed between Egypt and Israel. Egyptian president Sadat and Israeli prime minister Begin share the 1978 Nobel Peace Prize.		
1978	Under Prime Minister Begin, General Rafael Eitan becomes Israel's 11th chief of staff, launching an era of innovation.		
March 1979	Israel-Egypt Peace Treaty signed.	General Eitan officially approves Talpiot and gives initial instructions for implementing the program.	
spring 1979		Recruiting for Talpiot begins and plans for the program are developed. The first Talpiot class reports for duty in the summer of 1979.	
1981		Talpiot's base is moved from the Palmachim military base to Hebrew University in Jerusalem.	

DATE	HISTORICAL EVENT	TALPIOT EVENT	TALPIOT GRADS' ACHIEVEMENTS
1978–1982	PLO continues its campaign against Israel. Israel invades Lebanon again in 1982 and forcibly expels the PLO. Israel withdraws to a slim borderland buffer zone, held with the aid of the South Lebanon Army (SLA).		
1981	Ariel Sharon named Minister of Defense.		
1982		Israeli Navy is receptive to Talpiot cadets; looks forward to Talpiot help in modernizing. First Talpiot soldiers graduate from the three-year academic program.	
1982–2000	Ongoing war in southern Lebanon between the IDF, Hezbollah and other militias and guerrillas.	Talpiot cadets are sent to Lebanon for officer and combat training.	
1983		Computer science is added to Talpiot's curriculum.	
1983	Israel Space Agency founded by Yuval Ne'eman, who headed the Ministry of Science and was instrumental in getting Talpiot approved by the Ministry of Defense.		
1984		Talpiot begins allowing women into the program.	

DATE	HISTORICAL EVENT	TALPIOT EVENT	TALPIOT GRADS' ACHIEVEMENTS
1985	Hezbollah, a Lebanese Shia radical movement sponsored by Iran, calls for armed struggle to end the Israeli occupation of Lebanese territory.		
mid-1980s		Talpiot Professor Ariel Lorber devises concept and original proposal for Trophy active protection system for armored fighting vehicles.	
1985		Talpiot graduates become instructors in the Talpiot program, commanding at class level, for the first time. Talpiot graduate, Opher Yaron, becomes the first graduate to lead the program. Women are more aggressively recruited to Talpiot.	
1987–1993	First Intifada – Palestinian uprising against Israel in the West Bank and Gaza.		
1988	Israel launches its first Ofek satellite.		
1991	Missiles are launched at Israel from Iraq during the "Scud War."	Classes in military studies become mandatory for Talpiot students. Courses include instruction in the Arab-Israeli conflict, the modern battlefield and national security.	
1993/1995	Oslo Accords reached between Israel and the PLO.		

DATE	HISTORICAL EVENT	TALPIOT EVENT	TALPIOT GRADS' ACHIEVEMENTS
mid-1990s	Rockets are fired at civilian centers in the south of Israel.	Talpiot students suggest initial concept for Iron Dome defense.	
1993			Check Point Software Technologies co-founded by Talpiot grad Marius Nacht. Compugen founded by Talpiots Eli Mintz, Simchon Faigler and Amir Natan.
October 1994	Israel-Jordan Peace Treaty signed.		
1994	Era of suicide bombings begins.		
November 1995	Assassination of Prime Minister Yitzhak Rabin.		
1996			Check Point Software Technologies lists on the Nasdaq.
1999		Twentieth anniversary of Talpiot celebrated.	
2000		Talpiot program enlarged to accommodate almost twice as many cadets.	Compugen lists on the Nasdaq.
2001			Passave founded by Talpiot grad Ariel Maislos.
2003		Talpiot testing and recruiting is redesigned under Commander Amir Schlachat.	X Technologies purchased by Guidant. Talpiot grad Guy Shinar is closely associated with the company and with this first very large Israeli biotech deal.

DATE	HISTORICAL EVENT	TALPIOT EVENT	TALPIOT GRADS' ACHIEVEMENTS
2000–2005	Second Intifada – Palestinian uprising against Israel in the West Bank and Gaza.		
July–August 2006	Second Lebanon War against Hezbollah		
2007			XIV, founded by members of Talpiot Class 14 including Barak Ben-Eliezer and Ofir Zohar, is sold to IBM.
2008		Talpiot's thirtieth class begins.	
December 2008– January 2009	First Gaza War ("Operation Cast Lead") against Hamas.		
2011	Israel's Cyber War Bureau is founded as an advisory mechanism to the prime minister and to develop cyber defense. It is headed by Talpiot graduate Eviatar Matania.		Waves Audio Ltd., founded by Talpiot grad Meir Sha'ashua, wins Technical Grammy Award.
January 2012			Anobit, co-developed by Talpiot grad Ariel Maislos, sold to Apple.
November 2012	Second Gaza War ("Operation Pillar of Defense").		
July–August 2014	Third Gaza War ("Operation Protective Edge").		

A SALUTE FROM THE AUTHOR

Any time a book or detailed article is written about a sensitive military program, the writer owes a debt of gratitude to a lot of people who could not be named, but helped immensely with the research for the project. Israel has strict security rules in place to protect the identities of its pilots, espionage agents, military analysts, defense executives, officers, fighters and scientists. The IDF's Talpiot program is an all-star list made up of all of those components so necessary for an effective and formidable fighting force.

I'd like to thank the men and women from those ranks who helped me with information and research, and who simply helped me understand how the IDF machine works. While many could not be named for security reasons, and others did not have proper permission to speak to a journalist, their contributions were vital to this book.

This list includes men and women formerly of the Mossad who were so helpful with their time; executives from Israel's military contractors, large and small; former members of the IDF's spokesperson's office who were generous with their time but still needed to obey the rules of secrecy on certain subjects; current field commanders; air force pilots; former naval officers; several active Talpiot soldiers; and several Talpiot graduates now serving in various branches of the IDF and the IDF reserves.

They have served and continue to serve their country so bravely – commanding elite units in the field, always preparing for the next war and always trying to stay ten steps ahead of the enemies surrounding Israel.

Fortunately, there are many who graciously allowed me to use their names. Many thanks to the following Talpiot graduates:

Gilad Almogy

Mor Amitai

Matan Arazi

Yossi Azar

Uri Barkai

Oded Bar Lev

Ziv Belsky

Ron Berman

Saar Cohen

Arik Czerniak

Tal Dekel

Zvika Diament

Rotem Eldar

Barak Ben-Eliezer

Elad Ferber

Gideon Fostick

Marina Gandlin

Ra'anan Gefen

Kobi Kaminitz

Adam Kariv

Opher Kinrot

Giora Kornblau

Ophir Kra-Oz

David Kutasov

Gilad Lederer
Ron Milo
Eli Mintz
Marius Nacht
Dror Ofer
Amir Peleg
Barak Peleg
Avi Poleg
Boaz Rippin
Amir Schlachet
Haggai Scolnicov
Guy Shinar
Tal Slobodkin
Dr. Aviv Tuttnauer, MD
Opher Yaron
Guy Levy-Yurista
Ofir Zohar
Special thanks: Amnon Govrin, brother of Talpiot graduate
Oded Govrin (deceased)

Early Administrators/Organizers
Yoav Dothan, son of Felix Dothan, Talpiot's founder
General Uzi Eilam, former head of MAFAT
General Yitzhak Ben-Israel, former head of MAFAT
Colonel Benji Machnes, early founder, from the air force
Hanoch Tzadik, early administrator of the program, serving as
a psychologist

Early Observers of the Program/Former Soldiers
Odelliah Cohen
Meidad Muskal

Government Employees, Ministry of Foreign Affairs
Oren Anolik
Benjamin Krasna

Army Spokesperson's Office
Captain Eytan Buchman
Captain Keren Hajioff
Colonel Avital Leibovich
Libby Weiss
Lt. Col. Limor Gross-Weisbuch

Defense Contractors
David Ishai, Rafael
Noga Nadler, IAI

Industry Contacts
Martin Gerstel, Venture Capitalist
Yossi Gross, Rainbow Medical
Sharona Justman, STEP Strategy Advisors

Professors/Historians/Journalists
David Horovitz
Arieh O'Sullivan
Abraham Rabinovich
Amir Rapaport
Professor Jonathan Rynhold
Colonel Shaul Shay
Ronen Bergman
Ron Schleifer

Pop Culture Observer
Asaf Harel actor/producer/writer

The Staff at the IDF Archives
Israel Consulate, New York
Shahar Azani
Keren Gelfand

Acknowledgments

There is no way this book would have been possible without **Charlotte Friedland** and **Yitzchak Friedland**. Their patience in teaching me how to structure the book and their help in reworking it were simply invaluable to me. I will never be able to properly thank them. You are both wonderful editors and wonderful people. Thank you.

I want to thank **Ilan Greenfield, Lynn Douek, Kezia Raffel Pride** and **Esther Schwartz-Ivgy** of Gefen Publishing House for believing in me and in the book and of course for publishing it. I think Ilan really understood my vision for the book and my passion for the story from the first e-mail pitch I sent to him, many years ago.

Yehudit Singer, in Jerusalem, was a huge help connecting me with important people in Israel, searching for and finding impossible-to-find documents and translating them. Without her, I'd still be sitting on a cold library floor in Jerusalem with my English-Hebrew dictionary.

I'd like to thank many of the people at the IDF spokesperson's office, including **Colonel Avital Leibovich, Colonel Limor Gross-Weisbuch, Eytan Buckman, Keren Hajioff** and **Libby Weiss**. At the Ministry of Defense, I will be forever in the debt of several people who not only gave me advice, but served as valuable fact checkers…one even taught me how to walk between the raindrops; thank you.

Ronen Bergman, one of Israel's brightest military journalists, was extremely generous with advice and ideas along the way.

Hadassah Medical Center's chief public relations executive, **Barbara Sofer**, was always available for advice, counsel, friendship – and she could always be counted on to make me laugh.

Jeffrey Gewirtz and **Stacy Gewirtz** were terrific assistants, traveling with me to and from Israel. My father, **Michael Gewirtz**, was able to provide me with more research than I'll ever be able to properly organize and store; he was tireless in his efforts to suggest material he found online and in newspapers across the globe.

I want to thank **Robert DeFelice** for his help in graphically explaining my ideas for the cover so that Gefen's artists were able to produce the vision that I was unable to put into words.

Ron Schleifer of Israel's Ariel University was also very helpful with suggestions on how to turn my idea into a book, where to start and how to proceed throughout the way.

I've been extremely fortunate to work with some of the best people in the news business. **Mark Hoffman** has turned CNBC into the top brand in business news. He's made CNBC a place where all of his employees can honestly say it is a place where they're proud to work.

I especially want to thank **Nik Deogun** for his enthusiasm as I continued to research and write. Nik is one of the best and wisest newsmen I've ever met. His breadth of knowledge is never-ending; not just when it comes to content, but when it comes to management as well.

Jeremy Pink was exceptional for his initial encouragement at the beginning of this project. I want to thank **David Friend** and **Joel Franklin** for bringing me to CNBC.

This book would not have been possible without **Jonathan Wald**, who sent me on my first assignment to Israel as a producer and then kept sending me to cover war, peace and Warren Buffett's historic trip to the country in the fall of 2006. Those assignments gave me confidence not only to write this book, but to grow personally and professionally. Working internationally – including in the Middle East during times of war, and during rioting in Greece – with **Carl Quintanilla** taught me an enormous amount about truly working under pressure. The time I spent with Carl in the field were some of my proudest days as a journalist. I was also fortunate to work with many of the people in NBC's former Tel Aviv bureau, including **Gila Grossman, Paul Goldman, Dave Copeland** and **Martin Fletcher**, one of the most accomplished journalists to ever cover Israel. Traveling and working with CNBC's international correspondents **Michelle Caruso-Cabrera** and Senior Correspondent **Scott Cohn** were also experiences that had a big impact on me.

Without his knowledge, I used **Ben Sherwood's** book *The Survivor's Club* as a model for parts of this manuscript. Ben is a great story teller. I learned a lot from the short time I was able to spend with him and from his remarkable ability to tell a story and to let subjects speak for themselves.

Jim Rivas at Check Point Software Technologies was instrumental in helping secure key interviews and material.

David Raab, author of *Terror in Black September*, was exceptionally generous with his time and advice as I began to write.

Thank you all very much.